T0339537

Culturally Responsive Choral Music Education

Culturally Responsive Choral Music Education visits the classrooms of three ethnically diverse choral teacher-conductors to highlight specific examples of ways that *culturally responsive teaching* (CRT) can enrich choral music education.

Principles of CRT are illustrated in contrasting demographic contexts: a choir serving a sizeable immigrant Hispanic population, a choir with an African American classroom majority, and a choir comprised of students who identify with eighteen distinct ethnicities. Additionally, portraits of nine ethnically diverse students illuminate how CRT shaped their experiences as members of these choral ensembles. Practical recommendations are offered for developing a culturally responsive classroom environment.

Julia T. Shaw is Associate Professor of Music at the Indiana University Jacobs School of Music. Her research interests include music teacher education, culturally diverse learners, urban education, and sociocultural issues in music education.

Volume editors: **Vicki R. Lind**, University of Arkansas, and **Constance L. McKoy**, University of North Carolina at Greensboro.

Culturally Responsive Choral Music Education

What Teachers Can Learn From Nine Students' Experiences in Three Choirs

Julia T. Shaw

Routledge
Taylor & Francis Group

NEW YORK AND LONDON

First published 2020
by Routledge
605 Third Avenue, New York, NY 10017

and by Routledge
2 Park Square, Milton Park, Abingdon, Oxon, OX14 4RN

First issued in paperback 2021

Routledge is an imprint of the Taylor & Francis Group, an informa business

Publisher's Note
The publisher has gone to great lengths to ensure the quality of this
reprint but points out that some imperfections in the original copies may
be apparent.

Library of Congress Cataloging-in-Publication Data
Names: Shaw, Julia T., author.
Title: Culturally responsive choral music education : what teachers can learn
    from nine students' experiences in three choirs / Julia T. Shaw.
Description: New York : Routledge, 2019. | Series: Culturally responsive
    teaching in music | Includes bibliographical references and index.
Identifiers: LCCN 2019025093 (print) | LCCN 2019025094 (ebook) |
    ISBN 9781138587502 (hardback) | ISBN 9780429503900 (ebook) |
    ISBN 9780429995309 (adobe pdf) | ISBN 9780429995286 (mobi) |
    ISBN 9780429995293 (epub)
Subjects: LCSH: Choral singing—Instruction and study—Case studies. |
    Music—Instruction and study—Case studies. | Culturally relevant
    pedagogy—United States—Case studies.
Classification: LCC MT930 .S48 2019 (print) | LCC MT930 (ebook) |
    DDC 782.5071—dc23
LC record available at https://lccn.loc.gov/2019025093
LC ebook record available at https://lccn.loc.gov/2019025094

ISBN 13: 978-1-03-224045-9 (pbk)
ISBN 13: 978-1-138-58750-2 (hbk)

DOI: 10.4324/9780429503900

Typeset in Bembo
by Apex CoVantage, LLC

For Reid Michael and Mary Claire, who are among my most important teachers. Thank you for being a constant source of joy.

Contents

Acknowledgments

I would like to express my sincere appreciation for the teachers and students who contributed generously to this volume. To Mr. Moses, Ms. Rose, and Mr. Mitchell, thank you for graciously welcoming me into your classrooms and sharing your expertise. Your passion for music and commitment to your students is awe-inspiring. To the students who participated in this study, thank you for allowing me to learn from your valuable insights.

Thank you to editors Constance McKoy and Vicki Lind for the opportunity to contribute to this series and for your pioneering work on culturally responsive music education. Thank you, also, to Constance Ditzel and Peter Sheehy at Routledge for all of your assistance throughout the publication process.

I am grateful to Maud Hickey, Peter Webster, and especially Janet Barrett for thoughtful feedback on earlier versions of this work. Thank you also to Mary Goetze and Carlos Abril for all of the ways you have productively guided my thinking about cultural diversity in music education.

I would also like to thank my family for the many ways they made this project possible. My father, Dennis Dolken, has provided unwavering support during this and many other endeavors. My husband, Brian Shaw, served as a steady, encouraging presence, assisting in many capacities ranging from proofreader to cheerleader to coffee supplier. Thank you also to my children, Reid and Mary Claire, whose cheerful presence uplifted me throughout the writing process.

1 Introduction

Premises of Culturally Responsive Teaching

"I don't want to sing like a White[1] girl." This comment, made by a student during the first rehearsal of the newly established choir at Garfield Elementary,[2] took me by surprise. As a teacher who identified as a middle-class Caucasian, I was the only "White girl" in the classroom. Located in Chicago, the school served a student body that was 99.8% African American, with 88% of its students qualifying for free or reduced lunch (Illinois State Board of Education, n.d.). This school contrasted markedly with another in which I'd taught just months before in a suburb of Indianapolis, which had served an overwhelmingly White, middle-class student population.

Starting a new choir had generated excitement at Garfield, and the students were eager to begin singing together. All of the singers identified as African American, reflecting the school's demographic population. I began with a series of vocal warm-ups emphasizing the *bel canto* tradition of singing that had been emphasized throughout my education as a teacher. After addressing elements of Western classical vocal technique such as posture and breathing, I invited students to sing a five-note descending scale beginning from C5 on an [u] vowel. Because I then considered such exercises to be "routine," I was caught off guard when the singers laughed and appeared uncomfortable. The comment, "I don't want to sing like a White girl," came from Dameon, a seventh-grade African American boy. Unsure of how to respond in that moment, I continued with rehearsal. The students were willing to try everything I suggested, but weren't as engaged as I'd hoped and didn't appear to be enjoying the experience.

When I returned for rehearsal the next week, Dameon popped his head into the classroom just long enough to exclaim, "[Expletive!] I ain't gonna sing in no [expletive] choir," before running off down the hallway. I ran after him, frantically calling, "Wait! Can we talk? Tell me what would make choir better!" Halfway down the hall, he paused to explain that the repertoire I'd chosen wasn't the kind he was interested in singing. He observed, "You wouldn't know any singers I like. They didn't learn to sing in choir." The director of another afterschool program, having overheard, offered the names of several African American R&B and rap artists whose experiences had included singing in choir. As Dameon had correctly perceived, I was unacquainted with these artists, having not encountered them in my teacher education program or through personal experience. When our conversation concluded, Dameon was willing to return to rehearsal on the condition that I would learn more about the music he valued.

These early conversations with Dameon raised questions for me, some of which upended my own assumptions about "the right way to teach choir." What did it mean to "sound like a White girl?" How did the warm-up that prompted that comment reflect that sound? What, more specifically, did Dameon find objectionable about the way we'd sung that exercise? Who were the musical role models to whom students looked for inspiration? What kinds of music did my students consider to be relevant to their backgrounds, identities, or life experiences? What kinds of learning experiences would result in effective, meaningful, and engaging instruction for them?

All I had learned about choral pedagogy was gleaned in university environments where my experiences focused primarily on the Western classical tradition of choral singing, a tradition I continue to value and teach. During my early teaching career, the way I had initially learned to teach choir appeared on the surface to be compatible with the needs of my learners, the majority of whom were White, middle class, and residing in suburban communities. Yet comfortable and familiar ways of teaching seemed not to serve my students in Chicago, who were predominantly pupils of color, equally well. That is not to say that pupils of color, in general, wouldn't identify with the Western classical tradition or desire to learn it, but that my specific singers at that time considered different musical styles and genres to be more relevant to their experiences. To meaningfully engage Dameon and the many other wonderful students I taught in demographically contrasting communities across the city, it was apparent that changes to my practice were warranted. While I didn't yet know the educational term for what I hoped to learn, my interest in culturally responsive teaching had been piqued.

Culturally responsive teaching (CRT) is a pedagogical approach that uses "the cultural characteristics, experiences, and perspectives of ethnically diverse students as conduits for teaching them more effectively" (Gay, 2002, p. 106).[3] It is an asset-based pedagogy that builds upon students' knowledge and strengths while also broadening their intellectual, cultural, and musical horizons. While the central premises of CRT developed as one outgrowth of the multicultural education movement in general education, recent years have seen growing interest in how music education can be enriched through CRT. Considering the prominent role of singing in many of the world's cultures, as well as music's potential to serve as a powerful cultural referent, choral music educators are well positioned to create enriching learning experiences through CRT.

The term *responsive* emphasizes that CRT evolves in response to particular learners, implying a student-centered approach. CRT must therefore be understood in relation to the specific individuals for whom it is designed, and instruction that one student considers responsive to their cultural identity may not result in CRT for another. To attempt to offer a definitive "how-to" guide assumed to serve all students in all situations would therefore be misguided. However, stories of teachers and students engaged together in CRT can reveal guiding principles that can support teachers' efforts to design culturally responsive instruction for their own particular learners.

This book invites readers inside the classrooms of teacher-conductors whose work provides concrete examples of how CRT's tenets apply to choral music education. I present examples of culturally responsive practice from three teachers of differing ethnicities with whom I conducted research over a period of three years. Ensembles under the leadership of these educators offer a view of how culturally responsive choral music education unfolded in contrasting demographic contexts: a choir serving a sizeable migrant and immigrant Hispanic[4] population, a choir with an African American classroom majority, and a choir comprising students who identified with 18 distinct ethnicities.

Because of the student-centered premises of CRT, the voices of nine student members of these ensembles are foregrounded in order to elucidate how their teachers' efforts to practice CRT shaped their experiences of choral music education. The students offer a range of cultural perspectives, identifying as African American, Guatemalan, Honduran, Korean American, and Puerto Rican, as well as biracial and multiethnic.[5] In addition to illustrating the potential for CRT to engage and empower, teachers' and students' portraits illuminate challenges associated with implementing CRT and suggest possibilities for addressing them. This chapter introduces central premises of CRT, drawing upon the work of leading theorists in general education. These concepts are then further illustrated in descriptions of real-life choral classrooms that follow in subsequent chapters.

The "Cultural Fabric" of Choral Music Education

My student Dameon's perceptions of his experiences in choir can be interpreted as a response to the "profound and inescapable cultural fabric of the schooling process in America" (Boykin, 1994, p. 244). This "fabric" consists of beliefs, formats, perspectives, behavioral standards, and ways of constructing knowledge that are so deeply engrained in the structure and process of education as to be taken for granted as "normal" or "correct." While appearing on the surface to be neutral, this fabric has historically privileged White, middle-class students' orientations toward education, conferring distinct advantages upon these students as they progress through school. Conversely, the norms, values, practices, and codes of behavior legitimized by educational institutions are often incongruous with the prior knowledge and experiences of students of color and those of low socioeconomic status, dynamics which perpetuate social stratification (Apple, 1979; Bernstein, 1990; Bourdieu & Passeron, 1990; Delpit, 1995; Gay, 2010).

Choral music education in North America has traditionally been based upon Eurocentric frameworks, which have privileged the Western classical canon and its associated ideologies. Pedagogical and assessment practices based on these frameworks may present cultural incongruities to students whose musical knowledge and experiences are not centered in the Western classical tradition (Bradley, 2006; Carlow, 2004, 2006; Joyce, 2003; Kelly-McHale, 2011, 2013; Rohan, 2011). Further, a hierarchical orientation toward music that positions Western European ways of knowing about and participating in music as the "gold standard" of musicianship can be disengaging and disempowering to students from nondominant communities whose ways of knowing about and participating in music may not be valued, respected, or even acknowledged in schools.

Carlow's (2004, 2006) research exploring ELL (English language learner) students' experiences in a U.S. high school choral program illuminated threads in the cultural fabric of secondary choral music education that may be incongruous with students' experiences with singing. She coined the term "discourse norms" to refer to guiding principles and curricular traits that characterize the culture of a music classroom, including organizational structures, rehearsal techniques, and performance practices that are so commonplace as to be taken for granted as "normal." Examples of discourse norms prevalent in the institution of choral music education follow:

- Repertoire drawn nearly exclusively from the Western classical canon
- An emphasis on fluency with musical notation and deemphasis on aural learning
- Value for a specific Western European style of singing and vocal timbre and an emphasis on *bel canto* vocal technique
- Pedagogical frameworks with historical roots in Europe (e.g., an emphasis on Kodály, Orff, and Dalcroze approaches)
- A classroom culture that emphasizes individual accomplishment rather than collective effort (e.g., competition for solos, chair placements, roles in musical productions, etc.)
- Hierarchical organizational structures in which singers gain entry into progressively more selective ensembles through auditions
- Large performing ensembles as the preferred format for secondary school music programs

For music teachers interested in practicing CRT, a useful first step is to develop conscious awareness of discourse norms emphasized in our classrooms and then to recognize that these are not "neutral" but in fact reflect a particular cultural perspective that may or may not align with students' orientations toward music education.

Joyce's (2003) research illuminated "terms of engagement," which communicate to singers the ways they are invited (or not invited) to participate in singing practice (p. 1). She asserted that the terms of engagement traditionally emphasized in North American singing practice, privilege "Whiteness," which symbolically refers not exclusively to race but to an interlocking system of hierarchies and power relations involving class, gender, age, and so forth. According to Joyce (2003), "learning the 'White' way to sing" (p. 103) emphasizes the Western classical canon of repertoire, Western European vocal timbre, notational fluency, and individual rather than communal achievement. She cautioned that a nearly exclusive emphasis on these terms of engagement can alienate some people from the belief that they can sing altogether.

This discussion does not imply that there is anything inherently "wrong" with the Western classical tradition of singing. It is also not intended to suggest that Western classical music or associated pedagogical frameworks cannot be relevant to students from nondominant communities. It is a hierarchical orientation positioning any music as the most legitimate to study and perform, and an inequitable distribution of power that upholds some types of music and musicians as supposedly more valuable, that is problematic when the aim of music education is to provide equitable opportunities for *all* children to have enriching experiences with music.

What happens when the discourse norms and terms of engagement emphasized in educational institutions are misaligned with ways in which students engage with music? Teachers may inappropriately characterize learners as being uninterested in music or as presenting classroom management "problems" (Fitzpatrick-Harnish, 2015; Gurgel, 2016). These dynamics may also influence students' perceptions of themselves as singers or musicians, leading them to prematurely conclude that they lack musical ability or potential. Schools' devaluation of students' ways of being musical, whether tacit or explicit, may ultimately lead to singers' decisions to discontinue their involvement in choral music entirely (Joyce, 2003; Lamont & Maton, 2010).

The concepts of "discourse norms" and "terms of engagement" invite an interpretation of Dameon's reactions to his choral experiences not as "misbehavior" or "lack of interest" but rather as a logical and warranted response to an educational institution structured in a way that failed to honor or respond to the ways in which he was a musician. Drawing upon Giroux (1983), Chou and Tozer (2008) explained:

> The notion of resistance points to the need to understand more thoroughly the complex ways in which people mediate and respond to the interface between their own lived experiences and structures of domination and constraint (Giroux, 1983, p. 106). Stated differently, when people (including students) see their identities and experiences devalued by those in authority over them, they resist that authority. It seems clear that some teachers—and schools as organizations—are more adept than others at helping students learn mastery of new cultural codes without demeaning the cultural capital students bring to the school.
>
> (p. 11)

Dameon's perceptions of the terms of engagement operating within the classroom prompted him to literally run away from choir, raising the question of how many more students have been alienated by similar dynamics. CRT opens possibilities for ameliorating cultural incongruities in music instruction and honoring students' preferred ways of being musical.

Culturally Responsive Teaching: Central Premises

Several scholars of color are credited with developing the theory of CRT (Delpit, 1995, 2002; Gay, 2002, 2010; Irvine, 1991, 2001; Ladson-Billings, 1994, 1995; Villegas & Lucas, 2002), which evolved as a movement in general education in response to the significant opportunity gap[6] between White students of Western European heritage and students of color from low socioeconomic backgrounds. Many terms have been used to refer to ideas about why it is important to make classroom instruction more consistent with the cultural orientations of ethnically diverse students, including *culturally relevant, sensitive, centered, congruent, reflective, mediated, contextualized, synchronized*, and *responsive* (Gay, 2010). I will use "culturally responsive teaching" to refer to these ideas because the term *responsive* refers to teachers' responses to learners' cultural backgrounds and resulting strengths and needs, implying a child-centered approach. This student-centered orientation distinguishes CRT from approaches to music education in which the primary emphasis is on musical products or processes rather than on the child. This section describes theoretical frameworks developed by seminal authors in general education, highlighting concepts most useful for understanding examples of choral CRT presented in subsequent chapters.

Characteristics of Culturally Responsive Educators

Villegas and Lucas (2002) identified six distinguishing characteristics of culturally responsive teachers. Such educators:

> (a) are socioculturally conscious, (b) have affirming views of students from diverse backgrounds, (c) see themselves as responsible for and capable of bringing about change to make schools more equitable, (d) understand how learners construct knowledge and are capable of promoting knowledge construction, (e) know about the lives of their students, and (f) design instruction that builds on what their students already know while stretching them beyond the familiar.
>
> (p. 20)

The first of these characteristics, sociocultural consciousness, is defined as "an understanding that people's ways of thinking, behaving, and being are deeply influenced by such factors as race, ethnicity, social class, and language"

(Villegas & Lucas, 2002, p. 22). The process of developing or extending sociocultural consciousness requires self-knowledge of one's own sociocultural identity, including the various sociocultural groups with which one identifies according to age, gender, social class, race, ethnicity, language, sexual orientation, and exceptionality. Regardless of a teacher's cultural background, ongoing self-analysis regarding how cultural identity shapes one's own orientation toward education and how ways in which learners' orientations toward education may differ from one's own constitutes an important step toward CRT.

While such self-knowledge is crucial for teachers of any cultural background, ongoing exploration of this dimension of CRT may be especially productive for White, middle-class educators who presently comprise the demographic majority of music teachers in the United States (U.S. Department of Education, 2016). Teachers who identify as White may view cultural Whiteness as an absence of culture, or simply as being "normative"(Mazzei, 2004). However, cultural Whiteness forms a powerful lens through which educators view and practice teaching (Gere, Buehler, Dallavis, & Haviland, 2009; Haviland, 2008; Marx, 2006). As Ladson-Billings (2001) observed:

> Typically, White middle-class perspective teachers have little or no understanding of their own culture. Notions of Whiteness are taken for granted. They are rarely interrogated. But being White is not merely about biology. It is about choosing a system of privilege and power.
>
> (p. 96)

An ability to recognize and challenge ways in which racism and White privilege operate is therefore foundational to CRT (Hyland, 2005; Lehmberg, 2008). Saad (2018) has provided a wonderful free resource that can support teachers' efforts toward those ends.

Sociocultural consciousness further encompasses teachers' abilities to recognize power dynamics operating in educational institutions and how these perpetuate inequity and social injustice. A "meritocratic myth" is perpetuated in American society that maintains that schools are social equalizers in which students from any sociocultural background can succeed through hard work and individual merit. Socioculturally conscious educators recognize that, rather than presenting a "level playing field," educational institutions privilege learners who identify as White, affluent, and male (Villegas & Lucas, 2002). Lareau (2011) elaborates that

> the fact that many middle-class youth work hard should not blind us to the underlying reality that the system is not fair. It is not neutral. It does not give all children equal opportunities. Not only do schools vary, but in schools and other institutions that sort children into positions in the stratification system, some cultural practices are simply privileged more

than others. Our culture's nearly exclusive focus on individual choices renders invisible the key role of institutions. . . . The life paths we pursue, thus, are neither equal nor freely chosen.

(p. 343)

Villegas and Lucas's (2002) third characteristic of culturally responsive teachers, "commitment and skills to act as agents of change," emphasizes that culturally responsive educators not only recognize inequitable and hegemonic structures in schools and society, but also actively work toward dismantling them (p. 24).

The notion that culturally responsive educators maintain "an affirming attitude toward students from culturally diverse backgrounds" may seem self-evident, but Villegas and Lucas (2002) detail specific facets of an affirming attitude that merit music educators' attention and action. Culturally responsive educators:

> make it a priority for their students to develop facility with the mainstream ways so that they can effectively function in society as it is now structured. However, they treat the necessity for such facility as serving an instrumental purpose for their students rather than reflecting the greater value of those ways.
>
> (p. 23)

For example, choral teachers can teach sight-singing skills with the goal of equipping students to navigate opportunity structures as they presently exist (e.g., sight-reading components of auditions) but continue to affirm the skill of learning music aurally as equally valid.

Villegas and Lucas (2002) further emphasized that teachers with an affirming attitude toward students from diverse cultural backgrounds

> see all students, including children who are poor, of color, and speakers of languages other than English, as learners who already know a great deal and who have experiences, concepts, and languages that can be built on and expanded to help them learn even more. They see their role as adding to rather than replacing what students bring to learning.
>
> (p. 23)

To understand how this notion might apply within choir, consider the hypothetical example of a teacher-conductor working with a student who is an experienced gospel singer (one could substitute any genre here: K-pop, Bulgarian folk music, etc.). The educator might aim to expand this student's musical horizons by providing singing experience in genres new to the student but would not treat the student's preferred way of singing as in need of improvement, elevation, or replacement. Additional characteristics of culturally responsive educators identified by Villegas and

Lucas (2002) are discussed below as they relate to premises described by additional authors.

Premises of Culturally Relevant Pedagogy

Ladson-Billings' (1994, 1995, 2002) research was foundational to developing the theory of culturally relevant pedagogy,[7] which "empowers students intellectually, socially, emotionally, and politically by using cultural referents to impart knowledge, skills, and attitudes" (Ladson-Billings, 1994, p. 18). She developed the concepts of *cultural competence* and *sociopolitical consciousness*, which together with a focus on fostering high levels of academic achievement, comprise three conceptual pillars of CRP. Cultural competence "refers to the ability of students to grow in understanding and respect for their culture of origin" (Ladson-Billings, 2002, p. 111). Music teachers' efforts to promote students' cultural competence might include substantively incorporating music representing students' culture(s) of origin or reference into the curriculum, involving students' families in teaching and performing this music, and ensuring that individuals from students' culture(s) of origin or reference are respectfully represented in class materials and presentations.

Teachers' efforts toward developing sociopolitical consciousness "help students ask larger sociopolitical questions about how schools and society work to expose ongoing inequity and social injustice" (Ladson-Billings, 2002, p. 111). Learning experiences aligned with this conceptual pillar might include guiding students to recognize and challenge stereotypical thinking and assumptions; facilitating classroom dialogue about sociopolitical issues; engaging students in social critique through writing, composition, or multimedia projects; and assigning inquiry projects that involve taking action toward solving sociopolitical issues of importance to students.

Essential Elements of CRT

Gay (2002, 2010) identified five essential components of CRT: "developing a knowledge base about cultural diversity, including ethnic and cultural diversity content in the curriculum, demonstrating caring and building learning communities, communicating with ethnically diverse students, and responding to ethnic diversity in the delivery of instruction" (2002, p. 106). As these elements suggest possibilities for making music pedagogy more culturally responsive, a more detailed description of each is offered below.

Developing a Knowledge Base About Cultural Diversity

Just as music specialists invest time, effort, and seriousness of purpose in developing musical knowledge to inform teaching, so must they continually invest in developing a knowledge base about cultural diversity. This knowledge base must extend deeper than general awareness and recognition of cultural differences, to include "detailed factual information about the cultural particularities of specific ethnic groups" (Gay, 2002, p. 107). Such knowledge encompasses understandings about specific cultural groups' values, traditions, contributions, communication, and relational patterns (Gay, 2002, 2010). For instance, a teacher's understanding of particular ethnic groups' approaches to gender socialization or expectations for how children interact with adults in educational settings would hold important implications for instructing students from those groups (Gay, 2002). Rather than relying on assumptions about students' cultural backgrounds, identities, and learning needs, culturally responsive educators actively cultivate knowledge of cultural diversity.

Villegas and Lucas's (2002) fifth characteristic of culturally responsive educators maintains that such teachers "know about the lives of their students" (p. 20). These educators continually develop, refine, and extend their knowledge of the individual learners they teach and the educational, community, and broader cultural contexts in which they are situated. Culturally responsive teachers recognize individual variability within sociocultural groups and actively cultivate knowledge of the specific students they teach.

Including Ethnically and Culturally Diverse Content in the Curriculum

Culturally responsive educators design curricula with attention to ways in which cultural diversity is represented, misrepresented, or unrepresented in content and learning experiences. Gay (2002) identified three types of curriculum through which teachers can approach goals of CRT: "formal," "symbolic," and "societal" curricula (pp. 108–109). The formal curriculum is that which is sanctioned by school districts. The symbolic curriculum encompasses imagery in classroom displays, bulletin boards, decorations, awards, and so on. The societal curriculum encompasses messages, ideas, and impressions about cultural groups conveyed through media portrayals, which often propagate inaccurate, biased, and stereotypical views. Culturally responsive educators are consciously aware of the impact of such portrayals on their students and work to counteract them through their teaching.

Gay (2002) further warned that teachers must remain alert to and actively work to counter the following trends in formal curricula:

> Avoiding controversial issues such as racism, historical atrocities, powerlessness and hegemony; focusing on a few high-profile individuals repeatedly and ignoring the actions of groups; giving more attention to African Americans than other groups of color; decontextualizing women, their issues and their actions from their race and ethnicity; ignoring poverty; and, emphasizing factual information while minimizing other kinds of knowledge (such as values, attitudes, feelings, experiences, and ethics).
>
> (p. 108)

In light of these gaps in the formal curriculum, teachers can work to thoroughly infuse their own instruction with diverse content and perspectives; to fully contextualize that content in terms of race, ethnicity, class, and gender; and to explicitly address controversial issues. They can evaluate textbooks, repertoire, multimedia examples, and additional materials supporting the curriculum with a critical eye, making modifications and improvements when necessary to ensure that cultural diversity is represented accurately and respectfully.

Writing more broadly about multicultural education, Banks (2005) differentiated between four approaches to curriculum reform: "contributions, additive, transformation, and social action" (p. 246). In the *contributions* approach, multicultural content is limited to discrete cultural elements such as isolated heroes, heroines, and holidays. The *additive* approach features ethnic content and perspectives only as appendages to the curriculum. These additions are made without substantively revising the curriculum's structure. An isolated unit on African and African American musical traditions taught for Black History Month, without substantive treatment of these traditions throughout the curriculum, exemplifies an additive approach to multicultural music education. A *transformation* approach involves a more complete restructuring of the curriculum, thoroughly infusing it with concepts, issues, themes, and perspectives of diverse cultural groups. The *social action* approach extends the transformation approach, providing students opportunities to engage in decision-making about social issues and to take social action toward resolving them. The goals of multicultural and culturally responsive education are best realized through the transformation and social action approaches.

Demonstrating Caring and Building a Learning Community

It seems obvious that effective teachers would demonstrate caring toward their students, but Gay (2002) drew an important distinction between the kind of caring exemplified by culturally responsive teachers and "'gentle nurturing and benevolent concern,' which can result in benign neglect under the guise of letting students of color make their own way and move at their own pace" (p. 109). In contrast, culturally responsive caring "places teachers in an ethical, emotional, and academic partnership with ethnically diverse students, a partnership anchored in respect, honor, integrity, resource sharing, and a deep belief in the possibility of transcendence" (Gay, 2010, p. 58). Teacher caring has been a salient theme in several studies of culturally responsive music educators (Lehmberg, 2008; Robinson, 2006; Rohan, 2011).

Cross-Cultural Communications and Cultural Congruity in Instruction

Gay's (2002) fourth and fifth elements of CRT concern ways that classroom instruction can be made more consistent with culturally diverse learners' orientations toward learning. Discontinuities between the ways students from nondominant communities are accustomed to communicating, approaching tasks, and processing information and the processes emphasized in schools can present barriers to learning and engagement (Gay, 2010; Gurgel, 2013, 2016). To promote cultural congruity, teachers can intentionally develop approaches to instruction that build upon the knowledge, strengths, and prior experiences students bring with them to the classroom. For choral teachers, this process entails ameliorating disjunctures between ways in which students engage with music outside of our ensembles and the terms of engagement emphasized in our choirs.

The notion of cultural congruity does not imply that teachers should only present content and experiences with which students are already comfortable and familiar. Scholars have emphasized that CRT must broaden students' musical, cultural, and intellectual horizons as much as it affirms their backgrounds and identities (e.g., Villegas & Lucas, 2002). One way teachers can promote cultural congruity is by using culturally familiar elements to construct pedagogical bridges toward new learning, a process that Gay (2002) termed "cultural scaffolding" (p. 109). For example, choral teachers might use a vocal timbre with which students are familiar as a bridge toward learning repertoire in an unfamiliar language, style, and cultural context that features the same (or a closely related) vocal timbre. In this case, students would build upon a musical strength while engaging with material that productively challenges them.

Villegas and Lucas's (2002) fifth and sixth characteristics of culturally responsive educators provide nodes of connection with Gay's (2002) fifth element in that all three concern culturally responsive instructional practices. Examples of culturally responsive instruction in music education contexts have been documented by authors including Abril (2006, 2009, 2011), McKoy and Lind (2016), Lehmberg (2008), Robinson (2006), and Rohan (2011). This volume will provide further examples of culturally responsive instructional practices, highlighting pedagogical possibilities for choral teacher-conductors.

A Culture of Power in Music Education

In addition to making instruction more compatible with culturally diverse students' orientations toward education, CRT aims to assist students in navigating a "culture of power" that operates in schools and society (Delpit, 1995, p. 24). Delpit (1995, 2002) argued that educational institutions' approaches to literacy positioned standard edited English as a "code of power" to which students of different races and socioeconomic status received differential access, thus widening opportunity gaps in education. She further explained:

> (a) Issues of power are enacted in classrooms; (b) there are codes or rules for participating in power; that is, there is a "culture of power"; (c) the

rules of the culture of power are a reflection of the rules of the culture of those who have power; (d) if you are not already a participant in the culture of power, being told explicitly the rules of that culture makes acquiring power easier; and (e) those with power are frequently least aware of—or at least willing to acknowledge—its existence. Those with less power are often most aware of its existence.

(Delpit, 1995, p. 24)

Delpit's work suggests interesting parallels in music education, in which discourse norms associated with the Western classical tradition can similarly function as a code of power controlling students' access to opportunities (Bradley, 2006; Carlow, 2004; Joyce, 2003). For example, entrance auditions for choral ensembles often require students to demonstrate technical proficiency using traditional *bel canto* technique and to sight-read from musical notation.

Scholars have suggested that "code-switching," a sociolinguistic concept referring to "systematic shifting or alternation between languages" (Grant & Ladson-Billings, 1997, p. 44), offers a way for students to navigate opportunity structures while simultaneously maintaining a connection to their own culture(s) of origin or reference (Delpit, 1995, 2002; Suárez-Orozco, Suárez-Orozco, & Doucet, 2004). CRT, then, might facilitate students' ability to code-switch by helping them learn for which social contexts various performances styles, whether linguistic or musical, are appropriate. In this book, I use the term *style shifting* to refer to code-switching in a musical context.

Culturally Sustaining Pedagogy

Paris and Alim's (2017) edited collection offered a "loving critique" and theoretical extension of prior asset-based pedagogies including *funds of knowledge*, the *third space*, and *culturally relevant pedagogy*. The editors suggest that the "culture of power" in schools is evolving as society becomes increasingly multilingual and multiethnic:

For too long we have taught our youth (and our teachers) that . . . White middle-class normed practices and ways of being alone are the key to power, while denying the languages and other cultural practices that students of color bring to the classroom. Ironically, this outdated philosophy will not grant our young people access to power; rather, it may increasingly deny them that access.

(p. 6)

They further argue that the term "culturally relevant" does not go far enough toward critiquing power structures in educational institutions. Accordingly, they coined the term *culturally sustaining pedagogy* to describe teaching that "seeks to perpetuate and foster—to sustain—linguistic, literate, and cultural pluralism as part of schooling for positive social transformation" (p. 1). Additionally, the authors advance a view of culture as fluid and dynamically changing, and advocate for recognizing students' agency in shaping culture. While embracing theoretical premises contributed by these authors, I have chosen to retain *culturally responsive teaching* as my term of choice because the descriptor "responsive" emphasizes the student-centered underpinnings of this approach to teaching.

Research Basis

Portraits of culturally responsive choral music education presented in this volume are informed by a program of research carried out with three choral teacher-conductors over a period of three years from 2012–2015 (Shaw, 2015, 2016, 2018). The research context was an urban non-profit community children's choir organization that served 3,600 children, ages 8–18, through an auditioned mixed choir comprised of experienced high school singers, nine after-school choirs serving primarily third- through eighth-graders, and 60 public school choir programs rehearsing in demographically varied neighborhoods. I sought maximum variation (Creswell, 2007) in the cultural backgrounds of the teachers with whom I collaborated and the demographic composition of each choir. The resulting site–teacher–student combinations offered kaleidoscopic views of how CRT unfolded in varying demographic contexts (see Tables 1.1, 1.2, and 1.3). Brief descriptions of each choir site and its associated participants follow.

Table 1.1 Participants' Cultural Identities

Neighbor-hood	West Side			North Side			South Side		
Teacher	Mr. Moses			Ms. Rose			Mr. Mitchell		
Cultural Identity	Citizen of the World			Korean American			African American		
Students	Mateo	Kristina	Shirin	Sarah	Delores	Daniella	Zoey	Jazmin	Gianna
Cultural Identity	Puerto Rican	Guatemalan	African American, Filipino, Irish, Persian, Puerto Rican, and Baha'i	Korean American	Biracial	Mexican and Puerto Rican	African American	African American	Latina

Table 1.2 Demographic Information for Rehearsal Sites

Rehearsal site	Students' Racial Backgrounds				
	African American	Asian American	Latino	White/ European	Native American
North Side	6%	30%	23%	41%	—
West Side	14%	4%	73%	8%	1%
South Side	95%	—	5%	—	—

Note: These racial categories were used in the children's choir organization's registration process.

Table 1.3 Socioeconomic Information for Rehearsal Sites

Rehearsal site	Combined Family Income					
	$22,250 or less	$22,251– $45,000	$45,001– $75,000	$75,001– $100,000	$100,001– $150,000	$150,001 or more
North Side	13%	25%	14%	22%	12%	14%
West Side	46%	26%	10%	11%	5%	2%
South Side	—	—	—	—	—	—

Note: Socioeconomic information for the South Side Choir was not collected during the organization's registration process.

Mr. Moses and the West Side Choir

The multifaceted nature of Mr. James Moses's cultural identity led him to self-identify as a "citizen of the world." His Jewish parents left Germany at the outbreak of World War II, immigrating to South America where Mr. Moses grew up "as a Moses in Colombia." He was fluent in four languages, and had resided in such places as Jerusalem, Israel; Provo, Utah; and Chicago, Illinois. His choir was situated in a Puerto Rican enclave, where his instruction was responsive to a community with a significant migrant and immigrant Hispanic population. West Side Choir student portraits include those of Mateo, a first-generation[8] Puerto Rican migrant, Kristina, a second-generation Guatemalan immigrant; and Shirin, a multiethnic individual who identified with African American, Filipino, Persian, Puerto Rican, and Irish culture as well as the Baha'i faith. Mr. Moses's curricular and instructional choices provide examples of how a choral classroom can operate when learning is intentionally aligned with students' strengths, knowledge, perspectives, and experiences.

Ms. Rose and the North Side Choir

Ms. Lisa Rose, an ethnically proud second-generation Korean American educator, directed the North Side Choir in the same neighborhood in which she was born and attended elementary school. Her choir was the most ethnically and socioeconomically diverse of the three ensembles, with members identifying with eighteen distinct ethnicities. North Side student contributors included Sarah, a second-generation Korean American; Delores, who identified as biracial; and Daniella, who was the granddaughter of Puerto Rican migrants and the great-granddaughter of Mexican immigrants. Portraits of the North Side singers illustrate the potential for CRT to validate and affirm as well as challenges that may arise in the course of implementing CRT.

Mr. Mitchell and the South Side Choir

As an African American educator, Mr. Lionel Mitchell shared his cultural background with the majority of his students, all but one of whom were African American. Having grown up in a community adjacent to the neighborhood in which he taught, Mr. Mitchell's culturally responsive practice drew upon in-depth personal knowledge of students' cultural backgrounds and the community context. Two of the student participants at this site, Zoey and Jazmin, identified as African American. A third, Gianna, identified as Latina and was the only student who was not a member of the African American classroom majority. Mr. Mitchell's pedagogical responses to singers' learning needs provide examples of Ladson-Billings' (2002) notion of promoting "sociopolitical consciousness" (p 111). Further, his teaching assisted students with navigating a culture of power prevalent in the field of music without compromising their cultural identities.

In Chapters 2, 3, and 4, I describe how CRT unfolded in the West Side, North Side, and South Side choirs, respectively. I also describe some cases in which CRT did not unfold smoothly as well as learning experiences students did not receive as being responsive to their cultural backgrounds or identities. Chapter 5 offers interpretation and discussion of themes that emerged across the three choirs, and Chapter 6 discusses implications of these themes for teaching practice.

To develop descriptions of each choir, I consulted the following data sources: semi-structured interviews with three teachers and nine students (Fontana & Frey, 1994; Roulston, 2010), ethnographic field notes composed while observing choral rehearsals and performances (Emerson, Fretz, & Shaw, 1995), and a collection of artifacts (e.g., the organization's mission statement, teacher biographies, lesson plans, recordings of performances, and concert programs). Readers are encouraged to consult Shaw (2014) for additional methodological detail.

Some data generation techniques merit discussion in order to contextualize participant perspectives shared in upcoming chapters. To inquire about students' perceptions of the discourse norms and terms of engagement they experienced in choir, I engaged them in artifact-elicited interviews in which we discussed materials drawn from choral rehearsal and performance: recordings of singers they aspired to sound like, videos of concerts in which they had performed, printed concert programs, and so forth. Both teachers and students provided recordings of vocal models[9] they believed exemplified ideal sounds then commented on one another's recordings. Because only one teacher selected a vocal model that featured discourse norms associated with Western classical singing, I included an additional recording to invite students' reactions to those discourses: the Toronto Children's Chorus's (TCC) recording of Purcell's "Sound the Trumpet." Research evidencing the importance of vocal timbre and style to expressing cultural identity (Bradley, 2006; Carlow, 2004, 2006; Chinn, 1997; Joyce, 2003) informed my decision to use this technique.

Prior research has also suggested that cultural responsiveness, or a lack thereof, can influence students' perceptions of themselves as "musicians" and "singers" (Joyce, 2003; Kelly-McHale, 2011). To further investigate these issues, I inquired about how students defined the roles of "musician" and "singer," as well as whether they considered themselves to fulfill those roles (Kelly-McHale, 2011; Lamont, 2002).

The scope of this volume has intentionally been limited to the experiences of three teachers and nine students, bringing their perspectives into conversation with related research on culturally diverse learners' experiences in educational institutions. Referencing this literature is not intended to imply that all members of any cultural group share the same beliefs or behaviors. Considering the student-centered premises underlying CRT, it would be inappropriate for readers to generalize from the experiences of any one of these learners, applying similar pedagogical actions with students who appear to share cultural commonalities in hopes that CRT will result. However, the students' experiences can highlight questions teachers might ask and considerations they might make while designing CRT for their specific students. Teachers are urged to consult with their students directly and seek resources beyond this volume as they contemplate how best to approach CRT within their own classrooms.

Delpit (2002) asserted, "Since language is one of the most intimate expressions of identity, indeed, 'the skin that we speak,' then to reject a person's language can only feel as though we are rejecting him" (p. 47). I have previously suggested, and continue to believe, that

> replacing only a few words in author and educator Lisa Delpit's statement produces a thought-provoking perspective for music teachers to contemplate: "since music is one of the most intimate expressions of identity, indeed, 'the skin that we sing,' then to reject a person's music can only feel as though we are rejecting him."
>
> (Shaw, 2012, p. 75)

One impetus for this project was to explore ways that educators can honor the forms of musical expression with which students identify in choral classrooms. The pages that follow hold stories of teachers and students whose experiences illuminate possibilities for making choral music education culturally responsive.

Notes

1. Following a precedent established in prior literature, I will capitalize the term *White* throughout this book in recognition of "its status as a proper noun used to name a particular ethnic/racial group, recognizing the socially constructed, dynamic nature of racial categories. . . . By capitalizing this term, I purposely draw attention to the race, ethnicity, and power shared" by White people in the United States (Marx, 2006, p. 5).
2. All personal and school names used in this book are pseudonyms.
3. In this volume, culture is defined as "a dynamic system of social values, cognitive codes, behavioral standards, worldviews, and beliefs used to give order and meaning to our own lives as well as the lives of others" (Gay, 2010, pp. 8–9).
4. Following the recommendation of the U.S. Census Bureau (2011), I use the term *Hispanic* when referring broadly to people of Latin American or other countries of Spanish origins (e.g., Cuban, Mexican, Puerto Rican, South or Central American) regardless of race (see U.S. Census Bureau, 2011). When referring to specific participants' cultural identities, I use each individual's self-identifying language (e.g., Latino, Latina, Latinx, etc.).
5. All racial, ethnic, and cultural descriptors are students' self-identifying language.
6. Milner (2010) suggested that the term "opportunity gap" offers a more respectful and accurate way to describe the so-called "achievement gap" often referenced in educational policy. Rather than inappropriately blaming individuals for a lack of "achievement," the term "opportunity" directs attention toward "how systems, processes, and institutions are overtly and covertly designed to maintain the status quo and sustain depressingly complicated disparities in education (p. 8)."
7. While I have selected *culturally responsive teaching* as my term of choice, when synthesizing other authors' work, I will use the authors' preferred terms for related theoretical premises.
8. I use "first-generation immigrant" to refer to an individual who was born outside of and immigrated to the United States. "Second-generation immigrant" refers to an individual who was born in the United States to at least one foreign-born parent.
9. The term "vocal model" refers to "a standard or example of singing that represents a specific style, a behavior that is learned from sources within one's milieu" (Chinn, 1997, p. 639).

References

Abril, C. R. (2006). Teaching music in urban landscapes: Three perspectives. In C. Frierson-Campbell (Ed.), *Teaching music in the urban classroom* (pp. 75–95). Lanham, MD: Rowman & Littlefield.

Abril, C. R. (2009). Responding to culture in the instrumental music programme: A teacher's journey. *Music Education Research, 11*(1), 77–91. https://doi.org/10.1080/14613800802699176

Abril, C. R. (2011). Opening spaces in the instrumental music classroom. In A. Clements (Ed.), *Alternative approaches to music education* (pp. 3–14). Lanham, MD: Rowman & Littlefield.

Apple, M. W. (1979). On analyzing hegemony. In *Knowledge, power, and education: The selected works of Michael W. Apple* (pp. 19–40). New York, NY: Routledge.

Banks, J. A. (2005). Approaches to multicultural curriculum reform. In J. A. Banks & C. A. M. Banks (Eds.), *Multicultural education: Issues and perspectives* (5th ed., pp. 242–261). Hoboken, NJ: Wiley.

Bernstein, B. B. (1990). *The structuring of pedagogic discourse.* New York, NY: Routledge.

Bourdieu, P., & Passeron, J. C. (1990). *Reproduction in education, society, and culture* (R. Nice, Trans.). London: Sage.

Boykin, A. W. (1994). Afrocultural expression and its implications for schooing. In E. R. Hollins, J. E. King, & W. C. Hayman (Eds.), *Teaching diverse populations: Formulating a knowledge base* (pp. 243–256). Albany, NY: State University of New York Press.

Bradley, D. (2006). *Global song, global citizens? Multicultural choral music education and the community youth choir: Constituting the multicultural human subject* (Doctoral dissertation). Retrieved from ProQuest Dissertations & Theses. (AAT NR16043).

Carlow, R. (2004). *Hearing others' voices: An exploration of the music experience of immigrant students who sing in high school choir* (Doctoral dissertation). Retrieved from ProQuest Dissertations & Theses. (AAT 3152852).

Carlow, R. (2006). Diva Irina: An English language learner in high school choir. *Bulletin of the Council for Research in Music Education, 170,* 63–77.

Chinn, B. J. (1997). Vocal self-identification, singing style, and singing range in relationship to a measure of cultural mistrust in African-American adolescent females. *Journal of Research in Music Education, 45*(4), 636–649. https://doi.org/10.2307/3345428

Chou, V., & Tozer, S. (2008). What's urban got to do with it? Meanings of "urban" in urban teacher preparation and development. In F. P. Peterman (Ed.), *Partnering to prepare urban teachers: A call to activism* (pp. 1–20). New York, NY: Peter Lang.

Creswell, J. W. (2007). *Qualitative inquiry and research design* (2nd ed.). Thousand Oaks, CA: Sage.

Delpit, L. D. (1995). *Other people's children: Cultural conflict in the classroom.* New York, NY: Norton.

Delpit, L. D. (2002). No kinda sense. In L. D. Delpit & J. K. Dowdy (Eds.), *The skin that we speak: Thoughts on language and culture in the classroom* (pp. 31–48). New York, NY: New Press.

Emerson, R. M., Fretz, R. I., & Shaw, L. L. (1995). *Writing ethnographic fieldnotes.* Chicago, IL: University of Chicago Press.

Fitzpatrick-Harnish, K. (2015). *Urban music education: A practical guide for teachers.* New York, NY: Oxford University Press.

Fontana, A., & Frey, J. (1994). Interviewing: The art of science. In N. K. Denzin & Y. S. Lincoln (Eds.), *Handbook of qualitative research* (pp. 361–376). Thousand Oaks, CA: Sage.

Gay, G. (2002). Preparing for culturally responsive teaching. *Journal of Teacher Education, 53*(2), 106–116.

Gay, G. (2010). *Culturally responsive teaching: Theory, research, and practice* (2nd ed.). New York, NY: Teachers College Press.

Gere, A. R., Buehler, J., Dallavis, C., & Haviland, V. S. (2009). A visibility project: Learning to see how preservice teachers take up culturally responsive pedagogy. *American Educational Research Journal, 46*(3), 816–852. https://doi.org/10.3102/0002831209333182

Giroux, H. A. (1983). *Theory and resistance in education: A pedagogy for the opposition.* South Hadley, MA: Bergin and Garvey.

Grant, C. A., & Ladson-Billings, G. J. (1997). *Dictionary of multicultural education.* Phoenix, AZ: Oryz Press.

Gurgel, R. E. (2013). *Levels of engagement in a racially diverse 7th grade choir class: Perceptions of "feeling it" and "blanked out"* (Doctoral dissertation). Retrieved from ProQuest Dissertations & Theses. (AAT 3589385).

Gurgel, R. E. (2016). *Taught by the students: Culturally relevant pedagogy and deep engagement in music education.* Lanham, MD: Rowman & Littlefield.

Haviland, V. S. (2008). "Things get glossed over": Rearticulating the silencing power of whiteness in education. *Journal of Teacher Education, 59*(1), 40–54. https://doi.org/10.1177/0022487107310751

Hyland, N. E. (2005). Being a good teacher of black students? White teachers and unintentional racism. *Curriculum Inquiry, 35*(4), 429–459.

Illinois State Board of Education. (n.d.). *eReport card public site.* Retrieved from http://webprod.isbe.net/ereportcard/publicsite/getSearchCriteria.aspx

Irvine, J. J. (1991). *Black students and school failure: Policies, practices, and prescriptions.* New York, NY: Praeger.

Irvine, J. J. (2001). The critical elements of culturally responsive pedagogy: A synthesis of the research. In J. J. Irvine, B. J. Armento, & V. E. Causey (Eds.), *Culturally responsive teaching: Lesson planning for elementary and middle grades* (pp. 3–17). New York, NY: McGraw-Hill.

Joyce, V. M. (2003). *Bodies that sing: The formation of singing subjects* (Doctoral dissertation). Retrieved from ProQuest Dissertations & Theses. (AAT NQ78458).

Kelly-McHale, J. (2011). *The relationship between children's musical identities and music teacher beliefs and practices in an elementary general music classroom* (Doctoral dissertation). Retrieved from ProQuest Dissertations & Theses. (AAT 3456672).

Kelly-McHale, J. (2013). The influence of music teacher beliefs and practices on the expression of musical identity in an elementary general music classroom. *Journal of Research in Music Education, 61*(2), 195–216. https://doi.org/10.1177/0022429413485439

Ladson-Billings, G. J. (1994). *The dream-keepers: Successful teachers of African American children.* San Francisco, CA: Jossey-Bass.

Ladson-Billings, G. J. (1995). Toward a theory of culturally relevant pedagogy. *American Educational Research Journal, 32*(3), 465–491. https://doi.org/10.3102/00028312032003465

Ladson-Billings, G. J. (2001). *Crossing over to Canaan: The journey of new teachers in diverse classrooms* (1st ed.). San Francisco, CA: Jossey-Bass.

Ladson-Billings, G. J. (2002). I ain't writin' nuttin': Permissions to fail and demands to succeed in urban classrooms. In L. D. Delpit & J. K. Dowdy (Eds.), *The skin that we speak: Thoughts on language and culture in the classroom* (pp. 107–120). New York, NY: Norton.

Lamont, A. (2002). Musical identities and the school environment. In R. A. R. MacDonald, D. J. Hargreaves, & D. Miell (Eds.), *Musical identities* (pp. 41–59). New York, NY: Oxford University Press.

Lamont, A., & Maton, K. (2010). Unpopular music: Beliefs and behaviors toward music in education. In R. Wright (Ed.), *Sociology and music education* (pp. 63–80). Burlington, VT: Ashgate.

Lareau, A. (2011). *Unequal childhoods: Class, race, and family life* (2nd ed.). Berkeley, CA: University of California Press.

Lehmberg, L. J. (2008). *Perceptions of effective teaching and pre-service preparation for urban elementary general music classrooms: A study of teachers of different cultural backgrounds in various cultural settings* (Doctoral dissertation). Retrieved from ProQuest Dissertations & Theses. (AAT 3326036).

Marx, S. (2006). *Revealing the invisible: Confronting passive racism in teacher education.* New York, NY: Routledge.

Mazzei, L. A. (2004). Silent listenings: Deconstructive practices in discourse-based research. *Educational Researcher, 33*(2), 26–34. https://doi.org/10.3102/0013189X033002026

McKoy, C. L., & Lind, V. L. (2016). *Culturally responsive teaching in music education: From understanding to application.* New York, NY: Routledge.

Milner, H. R. (2010). *Start where you are, but don't stay there: Understanding diversity, opportunity gaps, and teaching in today's classrooms.* Cambridge, MA: Harvard Education Press.

Paris, D., & Alim, H. S. (2017). *Culturally sustaining pedagogies: Teaching and learning for justice in a changing world.* New York, NY: Teachers College Press.

Robinson, K. (2006). White teacher, students of color: Culturally responsive pedagogy for elementary general music in communities of color. In C. Frierson-Campbell (Ed.), *Teaching music in the urban classroom: A guide to survival, success, and reform* (Vol. 1, pp. 35–53). Lanham, MD: Rowman & Littlefield.

Rohan, T. J. (2011). *Teaching music, learning culture: The challenge of culturally responsive music education* (Doctoral dissertation). Retrieved from http://hdl.handle.net/10523/1865

Roulston, K. (2010). *Reflective interviewing: A guide to theory and practice.* Los Angeles, CA: Sage.

Saad, L. F. (2018). *Me and my white supremacy workbook.* Retrieved from www.meandwhitesupremacybook.com

Shaw, J. T. (2012). The skin that we sing: Culturally responsive choral music education. *Music Educators Journal, 98*(4), 75–81. https://doi.org/10.1177/0027432112443561

Shaw, J. T. (2014). *"The music I was meant to sing": Adolescent choral students' perceptions of culturally responsive pedagogy* (Doctoral dissertation). Retrieved from ProQuest Dissertations & Theses. (AAT 3627141).

Shaw, J. T. (2015). "Knowing their world": Urban choral music educators' knowledge of context. *Journal of Research in Music Education, 63*(2), 198–223. https://doi.org/10.1177/0022429415584377

Shaw, J. T. (2016). "The music I was meant to sing": Adolescent choral students' perceptions of culturally responsive pedagogy. *Journal of Research in Music Education, 63*(2), 198–223.

Shaw, J. T. (2018). Pedagogical context knowledge: Revelations from a week in the life of itinerant urban music educators. *Music Education Research, 20*(2), 184–200. https://doi.org/10.1080/14613808.2016.1238062

Suárez-Orozco, C., Suárez-Orozco, M. M., & Doucet, F. (2004). The academic engagement and achievement of Latino youth. In J. A. Banks & C. A. M. Banks (Eds.), *Handbook of research on multicultural education* (2nd ed., pp. 420–440). San Francisco, CA: Jossey-Bass.

U.S. Census Bureau. (2011). *Overview of race and Hispanic origin: 2010.* Retrieved from www.census.gov/prod/cen2010/briefs/c2010br-02.pdf

U.S. Department of Education. (2016). *The state of racial diversity in the educator workforce.* Retrieved from http://www2.ed.gov/rschstat/eval/highered/racial-diversity/state-racial-diversityworkforce.pdf

Villegas, A. M., & Lucas, T. (2002). Preparing culturally responsive teachers: Rethinking the curriculum. *Journal of Teacher Education, 53*(1), 20–32. https://doi.org/10.1177/0022487102053001003

2 Culturally Responsive Teaching in the West Side Choir

The West Side Choir served a sizeable migrant and immigrant Hispanic population, and the neighborhood in which it was situated was a thriving Puerto Rican enclave. Puerto Rican shops, restaurants, and community organizations lined the streets, including a Puerto Rican Cultural Center, the city's Spanish Action Committee, and the Puerto Rican Business Association. Public art displays referenced symbols of significance to the Puerto Rican community including the Puerto Rican flag, *El Morro*, an iconic Spanish fort in San Juan, and *el coquí*, a tree frog that serves as a mascot of Puerto Rico. Interspersed among thriving businesses, restaurants, and churches were vacant, boarded-up properties. Socioeconomically disadvantaged areas contrasted sharply with those that had been gentrified, recognizable by newly constructed, upscale condominiums. Referring to residential displacement, signs in windows read, "¡*No se vende!*" ("Not for sale!").

The choir's demographic profile (see Tables 1.2 and 1.3) reflected that of the surrounding community, with 73% of students identifying as Latino during the choir's registration process. The majority of West Side families (72%) were classified in the lowest two of six income brackets for the choir's tiered tuition program, with their combined annual family income falling at or below $45,000.

Teacher's Biographical Sketch

An energetic man in his 60s, Mr. James Moses was a self-described "citizen of the world." His Jewish parents left Germany at the outbreak of World War II, settling in Colombia. While he spoke Spanish at school, he grew up in a home that was "very European," and retained elements of German culture, including the language. Having resided in places ranging from Israel to Utah, and from Colombia to the Midwestern United States, Mr. Moses explained that his cultural identity was shaped by so many influences that he "didn't label himself." He was fluent in four languages (English, Spanish, German, and Hebrew), which he felt gave him "some perspective of the world." He held bachelor's and master's degrees, both in choral conducting.

Elements of Mr. Moses's Culturally Responsive Practice

Mr. Moses's curriculum was thoroughly infused with content and perspectives from diverse cultural traditions, and he strove to recreate the teaching and learning process emphasized in each culture studied as accurately as possible. The following field note excerpt offers a glimpse into his rehearsal:

> The rehearsals of Prelude, the West Side program's less-experienced choir, and Lyric, the more advanced group, overlapped by half an hour to facilitate interaction between singers with differing levels of experience. As Lyric students arrived, they sat among Prelude singers and joined them in singing "*Njengebhadi libhadula,*" a *Xhosa* folk song Mr. Moses learned from a colleague who traveled frequently to South Africa to research that country's musical traditions. Students did not refer to musical notation but listened carefully as Mr. Moses taught the piece orally. He coached singers especially on achieving appropriate vocal timbre for this piece. The choir learned accompanying physical movements, striving to perform each motion as presented in a multimedia resource featuring South African musicians.
>
> As the combined rehearsal drew to a close, Mr. Moses reminded the Prelude singers that their homework was to spend one minute each day reviewing the lines of the treble clef. Prelude singers exited chaotically as Mr. Moses led Lyric singers through several solfège patterns to focus their attention. They sang a melody to help them remember the location of the half steps within a major scale: "mi to fa and ti to do are the only half steps." Singers held their fingers close together each time they sang a half step. As a group, they practiced singing a chromatic scale.
>
> Next, the choir held sectionals to learn the first two pages of Hatfield's arrangement of "Apple Tree Wassail." Mr. Moses had written rhythms commonly encountered in 6/8 meter on the board. He isolated each, having students speak them using rhythm syllables. Then he pointed to the rhythms in various combinations, having the students practice alternating between them. Students located the rhythms in their scores, then progressed to practicing the melody using solfège syllables.
>
> Each section returned, having successfully learned their parts. The group stood in four circles according to voice part, combining the newly-learned harmony parts. Mr. Moses paired up students to help one another. He circulated among the students, sitting among them and leaning in close to assist. "Jayani, how are you doing? I'm going to sit right by you," he told one student. He pointed to her music with intensity, singing the solfège. Having accurately sung the first two pages, the choir concluded their work on "Apple Tree Wassail."

This rehearsal segment illustrates how Mr. Moses's students experienced repertoire from contrasting cultural contexts with their associated pedagogical discourses. Students rehearsed a South African piece through an aural learning process, with attention to singing with vocal timbre and movement appropriate to the cultural context. Immediately following, they rehearsed a selection of European origin, experiencing discourse norms traditionally associated with the Western classical tradition: sight-reading from musical notation, using rhythm syllables and solfège, and singing with characteristically Western European vocal timbre. Additional discourse norms prevalent in Mr. Moses's rehearsal environment are described below in relation to elements of CRT.

Developing a Knowledge Base About Cultural Diversity

Previous research with Mr. Moses (Shaw, 2015) illustrated how his experiences as a multiethnic individual contributed personal practical knowledge that supported effective cross-cultural interaction with students from diverse cultural backgrounds. The term *personal practical knowledge* describes knowledge that is "imbued with all the experiences that make up a person's being," including their experiences within varied communities of race, class, and ethnicity (Clandinin, 1985, p. 362). One of the most vibrant manifestations of Mr. Moses's personal practical knowledge occurred as he was selecting repertoire for a concert designed to engage the Puerto Rican community in which the West Side Choir was situated. To determine what music this specific community would find relevant, he sought recommendations from a Puerto Rican teacher colleague at one of the schools that fed his choir program. She suggested that he teach "*En Mi Viejo San Juan*," explaining, "This is a song that will bring tears to every eye in the audience." Mr. Moses summarized the song's significance as "a song of longing of Puerto Ricans for their country. It's a very romantic song, not of love for people but love to Puerto Rico" (Shaw, 2015, p. 211).

Although Mr. Moses was not Puerto Rican, as were many of the students in his choir, he shared an important commonality with many of them: the experience of having (im)migrated. Personal practical knowledge resulting from that experience led him to recognize the salience of "*En Mi Viejo San Juan*" to the community in which he taught. He could empathize with aspects of the migrant and immigrant experience, including disorientation, intense longing for one's country of origin, and the potential for emotional trauma resulting from family separations. When asked to elaborate upon what he understood about (im)migrant families' experiences that a teacher who hadn't (im)migrated might not, Mr. Moses responded:

> The feeling of cultural shock. The frustration is immense. They probably see the benefits of being here, but they miss their culture. I think there are many immigrant families that if you asked them, "Are you happy?" [Shakes head] They're not. Can they really feel like being at home? That's where the song "*En Mi Viejo San Juan*" comes from.
>
> (Shaw, 2015, p. 211)

On the evening of the performance, the resonance of this piece with the audience was observable. Attendees sang along with tears in their eyes and enthusiastically applauded the students' rendition. This episode illustrates how teachers who share cultural characteristics with their learners may be well equipped to connect with students as a result of shared knowledge and understandings.

In order to continually build his knowledge base of the values, traditions, and contributions of the specific cultural communities with whom he worked, Mr. Moses consulted with students' families:

> I inquire about whether there are musicians in the family. I love involving parents in concerts. That creates a commitment toward the choir and a strong connection with the kids. One father told me he plays the guitar. I said, "Bring the guitar in." He sang one song that was really beautiful, so I arranged it for the kids. They sang it, and they love it.
> (Shaw, 2015, p. 209)

His observations are consistent with those of Allsup, Barnett, and Katz (2006), who found that engaging students' families in their school musical experiences fostered a sense of cultural respect as well as ownership in the music program.

Designing Culturally Relevant Curricula

Mr. Moses's incorporation of diverse content in his curriculum was characterized by attention to the particularities of specific national, ethnic, and cultural traditions. He described his efforts to thoroughly infuse his curriculum with repertoire "from different countries which have slightly different flavors [so that] children can appreciate the change in the style of all these countries" (Shaw, 2015, p. 210). For example, pieces students sang in Spanish for one performance included a Mexican Baroque selection, a Spanish carol, and a medley of Puerto Rican *parranda* songs. Rather than including an isolated, token Hanukkah piece in his holiday concert, he presented pieces representing two specific ethnicities: "*Hannukah Lichterlech*," a Yiddish folk tune representing the Ashkenazic Jewish tradition, and "*Ocho Kandelikas*," a Ladino Chanukah song representing the Sephardic Jewish tradition. Each selection represented a specific ethnic, national, linguistic, cultural, or religious tradition, as opposed to educational arrangements published under vague pan-ethnic descriptors. Further, cultural traditions explored in Mr. Moses's classroom were those with which particular students identified, exemplifying the student-centered premises of culturally responsive curriculum design.

Demonstrating Caring and Building a Learning Community

Gay (2002) emphasized that culturally responsive teachers build learning communities in their classrooms. One way Mr. Moses accomplished this was by engaging students as peer mentors. Each Lyric singer sat next to a Prelude member, assisting them with everything from rehearsal etiquette to reading music. The resulting learning environment was compatible with the orientations of many students of color who "grow up in cultural environments where the welfare of the group takes precedence over the individual and where individuals are taught to pool their resources to solve problems" (Gay, 2002, p. 110). Kristina described the resulting learning community as being family-like:

> I feel this is kind of family, because we all know the songs we learned together. When Mr. Moses teaches us, he's very up close and personal. So leaving the choir just wouldn't feel right. It's like backing out on a group of family members.

The collectivist orientation characterizing Mr. Moses's classroom created an environment that students perceived to be caring, productive, and psychologically safe.

The organizational structure of the West Side Choir exemplified another discourse norm commonly associated with choirs: a hierarchical structure in which students progressed from non-auditioned to more selective ensembles. Mr. Moses's choir was divided by age and experience level into two groups, Prelude and Lyric. Research has documented how this hierarchical structure can serve to divide and alienate singers (for example, Bradley, 2006; Carlow, 2004, 2006). To attenuate this possibility, Mr. Moses fostered interaction between the two choirs by having them rehearse together and work in peer mentoring pairs, strategies that created a sense of community among his singers.

Even the physical arrangement of a choral rehearsal can function as a discourse norm:

> The director is positioned in front of the choir, which allows the singers to see the director primarily and each other only peripherally. All attention and focus move toward the director . . . this arrangement of bodies discourages horizontal interaction that might create community among the singers and detract from the director's control of the music-making.
> (O'Toole, 1994, pp. 18–21)

Conversely, Mr. Moses's use of physical space decentered the conductor as the primary focal point for students' attention. Rather than being anchored to the front of the room, stationed on a podium, or positioned behind a piano, he circulated freely among the singers, often sitting among them. He routinely positioned singers in formations other than traditional rows, deliberately promoting horizontal interaction that contributed toward building a learning community. These details contributed toward redressing power differentials between conductor and singers, fostering culturally responsive caring, and building a learning community within the choral classroom.

Cultural Congruity in Instruction

Through his instruction, Mr. Moses sought to ameliorate potential cultural incongruities related to notational fluency and vocal timbre. Elements of music theory comprised a salient pedagogical lens in his classroom as the previous field note excerpt exemplifies. However, he recognized that aural learning was a preferred learning process and strength for many of his students and provided balanced opportunities to learn music aurally when appropriate to the cultural context.

Provided that singing was approached in a healthy and age-appropriate manner, Mr. Moses believed it important for choirs to experience a range of vocal timbres and styles appropriate to the genre and cultural context from which each piece originated. Students sang Bulgarian music with its characteristically bright timbre, classical music with a pure, light, Western European sound, and gospel with a soulful sound and more extensive use of chest voice. While guiding students to sing with vocal timbre appropriate to each tradition studied bolstered the cultural validity of those learning experiences, these pedagogical moves also promoted cultural congruity by providing opportunities for students to showcase preferred vocal performance styles.

Mateo: "This Is the Music I Was Meant to Sing"

Mateo,[1] a 13-year-old eighth grader, described himself as "confident," "lovable," "helpful," and "determined." Although tall with a hefty build, he had not yet begun the adolescent voice change and sang with a pure, flute-like treble voice. As Mateo described, he came from a very musical family: "My brother plays the drums. I listen to his beats and we do music together . . . my dad does the guitar, and I do singing." Mateo's father and uncle were both musicians and were avid supporters of his musical endeavors. While musical opportunities were limited at Mateo's school, his participation in the children's choir organization coupled with an abundance of family support encouraged his positive identification as a musician. When asked whether he considered himself a musician, he replied, "Yes, I do because I really express myself through the things I sing."

Mateo's family migrated from Puerto Rico when he was seven years old. He explained:

> I had to move here because my dad ran out of jobs. My grandma had a house here and offered us the basement. . . . That was our opportunity, and we moved. I've been living here for the rest of my life, which makes six years. It was hard because I was in first grade, so I didn't really know what was going on. . . . It wasn't what I expected. I didn't go back to my home.

When asked to clarify what "home" meant to him, Mateo replied, "Where I belong. . . . Puerto Rico. I was born there and that's my island. . . . I love being there because when I'm there, I'm like, this is where I want to be." He explained that leaving Puerto Rico was an emotional experience "because the rest of my family lives there. . . . I really miss being with them. I'll see them again some day."

When asked to describe his cultural identity, Mateo definitively stated, "I consider myself Puerto Rican." He continued:

> I really like expressing that I'm Puerto Rican because not many people have the experience that I have. For example, speaking Spanish is one of the opportunities that I have. Eating a lot because I love to eat and especially over there, we get filled with food. It also means that I come from an island. . . . Over here, we have a lake. We [Puerto Ricans] call a beach, like a huge beach with an ocean. I got to see the Atlantic Ocean. I was six, but I still remember.

In Mateo's view, cultural identity relates to one's lived experiences: of the language, of the cuisine, and of living on an island surrounded by the ocean, for example. He summarized that being Puerto Rican "means that I have more experiences than other people. For me, that's what it is."

When asked to identify recordings of singers he would most like to sound like, Mateo chose three contrasting examples: a recording of "*Balulalow*" from Benjamin Britten's "Ceremony of Carols", Whitney Houston's rendition of "I Will Always Love You," and his own father's band's recording of "*Comprometidos*." His parents met when his father's band performed "*Comprometidos*" for his mother's *quinceañera*, and they remember that moment as the one in which they fell in love. When I asked Mateo what, specifically, about his father's voice he desired to emulate, he responded,

> His passion has a lot to do with what he sings. . . . I don't have the kind of passion my dad does. . . . I don't really have that much experience of that kind, so I can't sing like he sings.

The quality Mateo valued in his father's singing was "passion" derived from life experience.

Mateo described two experiences that vividly exemplified his positive reception of CRT. On these occasions, Mr. Moses centered learning experiences on music that was culturally relevant to Mateo, fostering connections between the curriculum and his lived experiences. The first involved learning and performing "*En Mi Viejo San Juan*," a piece Mr. Moses described as "a song of longing of Puerto Ricans for their country." Mateo described the meaning the piece held for him:

> That song actually reminds me of my island and how I moved and how much I miss it. Since my dad used to sing it all the time over there, when I heard we were gonna sing it, it really touched me. I was like, "Yeah, a

song from my island! Sing it for my island," and I almost wanted to cry. I wanted to go back, and I was like, "I miss you so much!"

Mateo also considered a *parranda* song his own father had taught the choir to be relevant to his cultural background. He explained:

> Because it does come from my culture, it expresses a lot of where I come from. I used to do *parranda* every single Christmas. I got my presents and my dad said "Hooray!" and then we went to my uncle's house, to my grandma's house. We went everywhere walking with a guitar, singing. . . . That's what we do in Puerto Rico. . . . That is one of my most favorite cultures and when I sang it, a lot of memories came back.

Both *"En Mi Viejo San Juan"* and the *parranda* song related to Mateo's "longing for home," a theme that described his attachment to and identification with Puerto Rican culture. Such a sense of longing is common among first-generation immigrants and migrants (Suárez-Orozco, Suárez-Orozco, & Todorova, 2008) and may be especially profound during holidays. Mr. Moses understood this emotional dimension of migration, which informed his decision to program a *parranda* medley as the final selection of his December concert. In so doing, he referenced a specific holiday tradition that held significance for the majority population in the community in which he taught.

Mr. Moses energetically took the microphone and introduced the choir's final selection:

> *Parranda Puertorriqueña* is a tradition that happens every year during the holiday season. People are in their houses and then they hear people singing in the street. . . . . Let's make believe that we're at home in San Juan, Puerto Rico [the audience erupts in spontaneous cheers] and—

Mr. Moses's introduction was suddenly interrupted by the sound of singing and Latin percussion emanating from the back of the hall. He feigned surprise as the children's choir lined the aisles, singing a lively call and response with the on-stage choir.

Locating Mateo on stage, I recalled a comment he had made in an earlier interview: "When I sing a Puerto Rican song in front of the public, I can sing it very well because my expressions blow off the roof!" Indeed, his facial expression was among the most dynamic of all of the performers as he sang the song his father had taught the choir (Field notes, December 15, 2013).

Mr. Moses's creative use of the performance space recreated the experience of a *parranda*, with singers approaching from a distance and surprising unsuspecting audience members who had been prompted to imagine themselves "at home" in San Juan. This performance was culturally responsive in that it went beyond simply singing a song in Spanish, assuming that the Spanish-speaking audience would relate, to referencing a specific cultural tradition that was relevant to the context in which it was presented. It triggered a flood of pleasant memories for Mateo.

Mateo developed a clear sense of Puerto Rican identity prior to his family's transition to the contiguous United States. Although he was born a citizen of the United States, several aspects of his migration to the mainland paralleled common experiences of first-generation immigrants: his unambiguous identification with his culture of origin, his sense of longing for his home in Puerto Rico, and his emotional experiences of separations and reunifications with family members while navigating the transition to the contiguous United States (Suárez-Orozco et al., 2008). By selecting music that honored Mateo's cultural heritage, fostering connections between the curriculum and his lived experiences, and engaging his father as a culture bearer, Mr. Moses created an environment that supported Mateo's use of music to express his Puerto Rican identity. Mateo's experiences represent a best-case scenario in which CRT opened validating avenues for self-expression, fostering positive connections between his musical and cultural identities.

Kristina: "I'm Kind of Half and Half"

Fifteen-year-old Kristina cultivated a casual, edgy sense of style, typically sporting baggy jeans, T-shirts, and funky knit hats. She attended one of the city's exclusive public magnet schools with a notoriously rigorous admission process. She offered the following self-description:

> I would think of myself as a very open person . . . as a kind person. . . . People have told me this and it will probably sound arrogant, but I think of myself as smart. . . . I think of myself as powerful, not only physically, but mentally.

Kristina sang in her school's auditioned mixed choir and studied voice privately, an experience through which she was "discovering herself as a singer." Her eclectic listening preferences ranged from classical music to rap and electronica. She frequently interacted musically with peers:

> We sing together randomly in the hallway. . . . We will just arbitrarily harmonize. We speak to each other in the melodies of the pieces we know. . . . A lot of my friends do beat box or they're in poetry slam, and we freestyle together. That's very cool. We have rap battles.

When asked to name a singer that she desired to emulate, Kristina's response was intriguing: "The first thing that popped into my head was nobody . . . I would never want to be like somebody else. I would like to sound like myself." She definitely identified as both a musician and as a singer, summarizing, "My mind just latches onto music whenever it can."

While Kristina was born in the U.S. city in which she resided, both of her parents emigrated from Guatemala. She spoke to the complexity inherent in describing her cultural identity:

> I say I'm a Guatemalan because although I was born here, my entire family was born in Guatemala. Technically speaking, that makes the blood in my veins Guatemalan. So just because I was born here, I think that kind of messes things up. So, I would say I'm Hispanic or Latin American. It's kind of hard sometimes, because people are like, "Well, what is a Latino? What is an American?" So I just say I'm Guatemalan; end of story.

Further complicating matters, her parents had yet another view of her identity:

> They call me *gringa*. They say I'm like a White person, because in comparison to them, I kind of really am a White person, because I was born and raised in the ideals and opinions of the United States, which makes me what they call an American. I still have an accent when I speak Spanish, even though I speak it fluently. If you hear a Guatemalan person speak and then hear me speak, the difference is very stark. So, I'm kind of half and half.

When asked whether it was important to identify herself as Guatemalan or American, Kristina offered a nuanced response:

> I'm not going to tell a person who asks me where you're from, "I'm from the womb of the Earth, it doesn't matter." No, you're going to say, "I am this. I am that." It gives you a sense of identity . . . it's part of your title. . . . In terms of racism, stereotypes, judgment . . . it is not important. . . . In terms of individualism, I think it is important.

In contrast to Mateo, who developed a clear sense of Puerto Rican identity prior to migrating to the contiguous United States, Kristina was one generation removed from her parents' transition to the U.S. setting. Her experiences illustrate how second-generation immigrant students "may be torn between an attachment to the parental culture of origin, the lure of the often more intriguing adolescent peer culture, and aspirations to join the 'mainstream' American culture" (Suárez-Orozco, Suárez-Orozco, & Doucet, 2004, p. 427). Responding to these dynamics, Kristina developed a "hyphenated self" integrating her identifications with both Guatemalan culture and American culture (Suárez-Orozco et al., 2004, p. 427), emphasizing that she was "half and half."

Kristina described one piece from the choir's repertoire that fostered a meaningful connection to her parental culture of origin: "It brought me to tears because it was it was almost like the Guatemalan national anthem. It's the song of Guatemala named '*Luna de Xelajú*,' and I was just so happy." Two aspects of Mr. Moses's instruction distinguished Kristina's experience with "*Luna de Xelajú*" as an example of culturally responsive instruction. First, rather than essentializing culture by viewing his choir as one homogenous "Hispanic" group (Erickson, 2005), Mr. Moses designed learning experiences based on specific national traditions with which individual students identified. Second, he attended to the "cultural validity" of learning experiences in his choir, striving to ensure that repertoire and performance practices were typical and representative of each culture studied (Abril, 2006, p. 41). That Kristina referred to "*Luna de Xelajú*" as being "like the Guatemalan national anthem" and as "the song of Guatemala" suggests a degree of cultural validity. The piece is a staple of the Guatemalan marimba band repertoire, a tradition Mr. Moses referenced by arranging xylophone parts for the students. Kristina believed their performance approximated the way the song would be presented in Guatemala and remarked that performing it "was amazing."

Classrooms operating under an assimilationist ideology[2] would seek to eliminate the hyphen from students' identities, encouraging them to adopt a "mainstream" American identity (Grant & Ladson-Billings, 1997; Skerrett, 2008). In contrast, the culturally responsive classroom in this study supported Kristina in maintaining a connection to her parental culture of origin. Such experiences may be especially meaningful to second-generation students, whose families may adopt a "leaky bucket" conception of culture (Erickson, 2005, p. 44), in which they fear a progressive loss of connection to their culture of origin with each successive generation. Kristina's experiences within a culturally responsive classroom supported her ability to maintain a connection to the Spanish language, form "diasporic attachments" (Inda & Rosaldo, 2002, p. 18), develop cultural competence (Ladson-Billings, 2002), and express her hyphenated identity.

Shirin: "If You Had a Pie Chart, My Culture Would Come From an 'Other'"

Thirteen-year-old Shirin described herself as "creative," "unique," and "an outgoing person." She delighted in putting together fashionable outfits and styled her long, wavy brown hair differently for each rehearsal. As vocal models, Shirin admired "strong, confident women" such as Adele and Demi Lovato, whom she perceived to be stylistically versatile. She described how singing distinguished her identity among her group of friends:

> I have a group of really close friends and we all do something different. Like, I have a friend who does cross country, and a friend who does soccer. I have a friend who does lacrosse, and a friend who does musical theater. I have an artist friend and then there's me. I'm the singer.

She further described her family's support of her musical identity: "I remember my grandparents saying, 'No matter what you do, we'll always be supportive. We'll always push you to do your best at what that is,' and I chose music. I chose singing."

Shirin was born and raised in the U.S. city in which she resided. While her primary language was English, she also spoke Spanish with her stepfather at home and at the language immersion school she attended. When Shirin described her cultural identity, a multifaceted picture emerged: "I'll start with my grandparents from my mom's side. My papa is Irish and my grandma is Persian. . . . My dad is African American and Filipino. So, I'm all that." She also considered religion to be a salient dimension of her cultural identity: "I grew up as a Baha'i. . . . I would consider it a culture and a way of life where we believe and we study about all cultures and religions." Shirin considered herself to be multicultural, with each of those cultures (Irish, Persian, African American, Filipino, and the Baha'i faith) comprising an important dimension of her identity.

Shirin recognized that Mr. Moses's repertoire choices were often responsive to the majority culture of the classroom and neighborhood:

> We sing Spanish songs because the majority of the people in the choir come from a Hispanic background, either like Mexican, Puerto Rican, Colombian, Cuban, any of that, and our neighborhood is I guess considered, in the eyes of other people, a Hispanic neighborhood. Mr. Moses is Colombian, so he knows a lot about it. . . . A lot of the parents are also Hispanic.

However, she had not personally had opportunities to express her cultural identity musically.

Julia: Do you think it's important to identify yourself as a Baha'i? As African American? As Irish? As . . .

Shirin: Of course I think it's important. I think it is because everyone is different and you should feel like you can express who you are to anybody.

Julia: Do you think music plays into that at all for you?

Shirin: For me personally, I don't think so. Because I have yet to . . . [hesitating] I don't know a Persian or Irish [song] that I've sung, but I'm sure they're out there somewhere.

While an occasion had yet to arise for her to sing music relating to one of her cultures of origin or reference, she related, "It'd be cool [to sing] a Persian piece or an Irish-themed type of music. . . . It'd be cool to explore and teach people. I'd feel really proud to . . . help them I guess."

While Shirin described the value of students learning music that represented their own cultural heritage, she consistently reported that she had not personally had such opportunities. Finally, as we neared the conclusion of Shirin's final interview, she returned to a question she had earlier dismissed as irrelevant, having made a realization about the *parranda* medley the choir had recently performed:

> I just remembered—my stepfather is Puerto Rican. [He] told me that he did a *parranda* once in Puerto Rico and a lot of his friends did it, so we had a nice conversation about that. He saw me play the *guiro* and he knew the song. He was singing it on the way back from the concert in the car, and I was like, "You know that song?" He was like, "Of course I do, it's from Puerto Rico." And I was like, "Oh yeah. That's right." So, it was really cool . . . it connected us.

As she elaborated on their post-concert conversation, she revealed yet another facet of her multiethnic identity that she had not previously discussed:

> My stepdad grew up and was born in Puerto Rico. He lived there for eight years. He has family there and I've been there twice. He really loves it there and I really love it there. We have art from Puerto Rico all over the house. Some relatives who also live here are Puerto Rican. We live in a Puerto Rican neighborhood, which is a great way to kind of enhance the culture and religion. I remember when I was in Kindergarten, [people would ask:] "Oh, so what are you? Are you Mexican? Are you something like that?" I used to tell them that I was Puerto Rican because I'd grown up with my stepfather, who really taught me cool things about it. After a while I realized that I actually wasn't, but in a way, I would consider myself Puerto Rican because I know the culture. I've been there. I know the people and I love Puerto Rico.

Although Shirin did not receive Mr. Moses's repertoire selections as being particularly responsive to her cultural background, a repertoire choice driven by his responsiveness to the classroom majority did ultimately result in an unexpected connection to one facet of her cultural identity. She summarized the piece's cultural relevance in this way: "It didn't come from my blood background, but it came from the background of someone I've known basically my whole life." Her experience of CRT did ultimately forge a connection between her musical and cultural identities, although the pedagogical pathway to creating that connection was unpredictable.

For Shirin, the process of adolescent self-discovery involved making sense of her multiracial and multicultural identity, which encompassed attachments to African American, Filipino, Irish, and Persian culture as well as the Baha'i faith. Previous research has emphasized that biracial or multiracial children's parents may not themselves be biracial or multiracial, potentially posing challenges for families as they discuss race, ethnicity, and identity (Root, 2004). For these and for all students, schools and community organizations can fill an important role as sites for adolescents' identity construction, complementing dialogue and guidance offered in students' homes (Olneck, 2004; Root, 2004; Suárez-Orozco et al., 2004). The West Side Choir fulfilled that role for Shirin, affording opportunities to explore, express, and integrate various facets of her multiethnic identity. While the complexity of her identity initially prevented her from believing that Mr. Moses's instruction was responsive to her culture in particular, the choir's performance of Puerto Rican music prompted dialogue with her stepfather leading to a realization that her experiences growing up with a Puerto Rican stepfather in a Puerto Rican community were relevant to her identity. Her experiences with CRT broadened her conception of her cultural identity, which was previously biologically driven, and encouraged exploration of lesser-known facets of her multiethnic identity.

CRT and Intersections Between Students' Musical and Cultural Identities

In contrast to studies in which a lack of cultural responsiveness alienated students from the belief that they were singers (Joyce, 2003) or musicians (Kelly-McHale, 2011, 2013), students in the West Side Choir assuredly considered themselves to be both. Mr. Moses rejected the notion of a single ideal choral sound, and his openness toward multiple valid ways of singing was mirrored in his students' varied vocal models. For example, Mateo's preferred vocal models included music historically deemed legitimate by academic institutions (the Western classical tradition), mainstream adolescent peer culture (popular music), and his parental culture of origin (his own father's singing). That students selected family members and themselves as models representing a desirable standard of singing is significant. Had the Western classical style of singing been privileged as a dominant discourse, students may have concluded that their family members' or their own ways of singing were invalid (Joyce, 2003). To the contrary, the culturally responsive learning environment Mr. Moses created affirmed students' musical identities.

Rather than asserting that any particular vocal style, timbre, or performance practice was correct in an absolute sense, Mr. Moses guided students to discover the musical situations for which each was appropriate. As a result, his students developed an ability to fluidly shift between vocal styles appropriate to a variety of culturally and stylistically diverse repertoire. Students perceived the ability to style shift to be an important dimension of musicianship as well as a form of advantageous capital for being promoted to more advanced choirs within the organization. Shirin described style shifting as something she has "grown to love":

> It's fascinating, but it's also hard because there's different ways that Mr. Moses wants us to sing. There's more classical where you have to stand up and all make an "O" shape, but then in Bulgarian he says, "Just let

loose and open your mouth." . . . One minute we're doing a classical song and you tune your mind to sing very proper, but then in Bulgarian music you kind of have to tune your mind to do that too. . . . It's something I've grown to love.

The systematic style shifting Mr. Moses encouraged opened possibilities for students to develop "transcultural identities," characterized by fluid navigation between two or more cultures (Suárez-Orozco et al., 2004, p. 430). In this way, CRT fostered accommodation without assimilation, allowing students to navigate organizational and societal opportunity structures while continuing to identify with their culture(s) of reference.

Fulfilling a bridging function between students' homes and educational institutions was an additional means by which CRT fostered intersections between students' musical and cultural identities. Students' experiences in choir catalyzed interactions with their families that strengthened their cultural identities, and students' musical and cultural experiences at home informed classroom instruction. This finding carries significance in light of research evidencing cultural gulfs between students' musical experiences inside and outside of the school music domain (Carlow, 2004, 2006; Kelly-McHale, 2011, 2013; Lum, 2007; Lum & Campbell, 2009).

Students' Perceptions of Culturally Responsive Teaching

Generally, Mr. Moses's students perceived his instruction to be responsive to cultural diversity. Their perceptions revolved around three themes: developing cultural competence, expanding cultural horizons, and enhancing cultural validity. Students appreciated opportunities Mr. Moses provided to study music representative of their own cultural backgrounds. They described these experiences as deepening their understanding of and appreciation for their own cultures, which corresponded to Ladson-Billings's (2002) conception of cultural competence. For Kristina, such opportunities were motivating:

> If someone is from Guatemala and you're singing what's important to that [Guatemalan culture], you're not gonna blow it off. . . . You're gonna do everything you can to make it sound great. And you connect with it. It's fun. . . . "The song's from Mexico, I'm from Mexico—hey, that's cool!" I feel like that's a motivational thing.

For Shirin, these occasions fostered a sense of pride:

> You have this pride in you that, "Wow, I know where this song came from. My grandparents used to sing this to me." . . . You can tell people about it and for once, you know what's going on musically. You're more familiar with the material and you feel proud to be part of that.

For Mateo, opportunities to sing Puerto Rican music were validating, producing a visceral response: "When I sing Puerto Rican music, it's like it belongs to me. It's like that feeling in my veins and it's like I hear my heart beating. Like this is the music I was meant to sing."

While students valued learning opportunities that affirmed their cultural backgrounds, they raised a concern that focusing exclusively on the cultural backgrounds of students in a given classroom would result in curricular bias. Students were especially eager to respond to one particular question: Do you think the teacher should consider the cultural identities of the students in the class when they're making important decisions about what and how to teach? Kristina responded:

> You have to learn about your students . . . but I don't think a teacher goes, "Oh, 50% of my class is Mexican so I'll teach this way because they must understand more if I do." I think that to a certain extent, that's being biased . . . being more closed-minded than open-minded if you generalize your lessons based on someone's culture.

Shirin was also concerned that a curriculum based on students' personal cultural backgrounds would be too limiting: "Why focus on what they already know and are very familiar with [rather] than look at these whole undiscovered cultures and their music?" Mateo suggested a compromise: "It would be nice for [teachers] to focus a little bit on your culture and then a lot more on other cultures, because as you learn about other cultures, you want to learn more about your culture." Students' insights closely aligned with those of leading theorists on culturally responsive pedagogy, who have emphasized that CRT must expand students' horizons as much as it validates their own backgrounds (e.g., Gay, 2002; Ladson-Billings, 1994; Villegas & Lucas, 2002).

Mr. Moses's frequent consultation with culture bearers, or representatives of each culture studied (Campbell, 2004), was a culturally responsive practice to which his students reacted positively. Mateo's own father served as a culture bearer, creating a meaningful experience for him:

> It made me feel proud of having a dad that can sing and actually brought a song to the choir. . . . He played the guitar, he sang with us for one of the concerts, and it was really great. We were having a lot of fun with my dad.

Mateo further explained that working with culture bearers provided opportunities for students to

> get some thoughts and words from actual people that come from that place and that actually sing the song every day. . . . That actually teaches us more about their culture and more about stuff they know, [which leads to] more experience, knowing more people, learning new languages . . . experiencing what they have experienced already.

His explanation of the value of consulting with culture bearers highlights the connections CRT creates between musical and lived experiences. CRT connects students with "actual people" who "actually sing the songs," providing a window into "what they have experienced."

As Joyce (2003) cautioned, merely including diverse music in the curriculum cannot guarantee meaningful or positive learning experiences:

> Music and vocal techniques of the "Other" featured in multicultural projects are always at risk of being exoticized, exploited, or appropriated. At the hands of ill-prepared teachers, it is also at risk of being distorted, misrepresented and diminished. . . . Visibility and inclusion require collaboration and strategic planning if it is to lessen or avoid damage.
>
> (pp. 256–257)

Consulting with culture bearers is one means by which teachers can maximize the cultural validity of learning experiences while minimizing the risks Joyce described. As Mateo attested, engaging students' family members as culture bearers and designing lessons based on their "funds of knowledge" (Moll & González, 2004) can result in potent learning.

Students' Perceived Barriers to CRT

Even in a classroom students considered to be culturally responsive, they identified barriers to practicing CRT. First, they considered the complexity involved in determining what music students consider culturally relevant to present an implementation challenge. As they observed, students' cultural identities encompass connections with multiple social groups that interact in complex ways (Erickson, 2005), making it difficult for teachers to identify what music or learning experiences they will find culturally relevant. Shirin was herself challenged to identify repertoire or musical experiences that aligned with her multifaceted identity and recognized the challenge this would present to her teacher.

The complexities involved in identifying what experiences constitute CRT for one student are compounded when attempting to design CRT for each of the individuals in a classroom. Shirin described how experiences that would be responsive to the majority culture in her classroom would not necessarily be relevant to her given her multiethnic background:

> If you were to have a pie chart that said each [culture] . . . you know how there's always that little slit that's like "other?" I think that my culture and what I believe in would come from an "other." So I think that our teacher does focus on the cultures of this choir because a lot of the people from our choir are from a Hispanic background and are Mexican, Colombian, Guatemalan, all of that cool stuff . . . but not everyone in the choir is like that.

While responding to the classroom majority presents a logical point of departure for practicing CRT, it can result in missed opportunities for students like Shirin, who repeatedly remarked that she "had yet to have had an opportunity" to study music with which she identified culturally. Issues such as these led students to question whether it is possible to practice CRT equitably given constraints on instructional time and the difficulties inherent in attempting to address every conceivable culture. They voiced a related concern that peers whose cultures remained unaddressed would feel excluded.

Kristina's experience presented a conundrum in that even her positive experience performing *"Luna de Xelajú,"* which she described as fostering a meaningful connection to her parental culture of origin, was insufficient for her to perceive her choral experience in general to be responsive to her cultural background. When asked, "Do you have opportunities in choir to learn about or perform Guatemalan music?" she responded with a definitive "No," emphasizing, "We've only done one Guatemalan song in the three years I've been here." Furthermore, she did not assume Mr. Moses's decision to teach *"Luna de Xelajú"* had been motivated by an attempt to respond to her culture in particular. When asked if her teacher had chosen the piece because he was aware of her cultural background, Kristina quickly dismissed the possibility, stating, "No. He was just like, I bet you'll like this song, and I'm like, why?" Her case suggests that a single isolated instance of CRT may be insufficient for students to perceive their music instruction in general to be culturally responsive.

Promising Practices and Paradoxes

The West Side singers' perspectives suggest that a content integration approach to CRT centered on repertoire teachers assume will correspond with students' cultural backgrounds will not necessarily result in students feeling culturally recognized or validated (Karlsen, 2013). Selecting repertoire that corresponds to students' cultural backgrounds is far from a straightforward task, and potential exists for students to be alienated by instruction based on misguided teacher assumptions about musical experiences they will consider relevant. Additionally, responding to individual students' cultures through a rotating schedule of repertoire-based experiences requires a significant investment of instructional time and risks marginalizing students whose backgrounds are not addressed, dynamics of which participants in this study were acutely aware. Their insights illuminate a paradox whereby an approach to teaching intended to foster recognition of diverse cultural groups may instead lead to marginalization if not practiced equitably. Potential barriers to CRT that teachers can learn to proactively anticipate, as well as possibilities for ameliorating them, are discussed in subsequent chapters and summarized in Chapter 5.

Despite the potential barriers, Mateo's experiences singing Puerto Rican music illustrate that affirming experiences can result from teachers' attempts to design culturally responsive instruction. To increase the likelihood of creating validating experiences for students, teachers must go beyond addressing the important but insufficient content integration dimension of CRT. Effective culturally responsive teaching also encompasses basing instruction on detailed knowledge of students' biographies and identities, ensuring the cultural validity of content and learning experiences (Abril, 2006), involving students' families in their education (Allsup et al., 2006; Moll & González, 2004), addressing sociopolitical issues and tensions (Abril, 2011; Ladson-Billings, 2002), and honoring students' expert knowledge in the classroom (Delpit, 1995). As the West Side singers' experiences illustrate, CRT affords opportunities to bridge students' home and school experiences, expand their musical and cultural horizons, and affirm their identities, using the music students believe they were "meant to sing."

Notes

1. The three student portraits and subsequent discussion of overarching themes in the West Side Choir are reprinted with permission from Shaw, J. T. (2016). "The music I was meant to sing": Adolescent choral students' perceptions of culturally responsive pedagogy. *Journal of Research in Music Education, 63*(2), 198–223. © 2016 by National Association for Music Education (formerly MENC). Reprinted with permission.
2. Assimilation refers to "a process by which a person or group is absorbed into the social structures and cultural life of another person, group, or society" (Grant & Ladson-Billings, 1997, p. 24). Within the context of U.S. society, this process requires racial and ethnic groups to abandon their culture of origin in order to embrace the norms of middle-class, White, mainstream culture (see also Skerrett, 2008).

References

Abril, C. R. (2006). Music that represents culture: Selecting music with integrity. *Music Educators Journal, 93*(1), 38–45. https://doi.org/10.1177/002743210609300122

Abril, C. R. (2011). Opening spaces in the instrumental music classroom. In A. Clements (Ed.), *Alternative approaches to music education* (pp. 3–14). Lanham, MD: Rowman & Littlefield.

Allsup, R. E., Barnett, A. C., & Katz, E. J. (2006). Musical heritage: Celebrating families through music. In C. Frierson-Campbell (Ed.), *Teaching music in the urban classroom: A guide to leadership, teacher education, and reform* (Vol. 2, pp. 123–136). Lanham, MD: Rowman & Littlefield.

Bradley, D. (2006). *Global song, global citizens? Multicultural choral music education and the community youth choir: Constituting the multicultural human subject* (Doctoral dissertation). Retrieved from ProQuest Dissertations & Theses. (AAT NR16043).

Campbell, P. S. (2004). *Teaching music globally: Experiencing music, expressing culture.* New York, NY: Oxford University Press.

Carlow, R. (2004). *Hearing others' voices: An exploration of the music experience of immigrant students who sing in high school choir* (Doctoral dissertation). Retrieved from ProQuest Dissertations & Theses. (AAT 3152852).

Carlow, R. (2006). Diva Irina: An English language learner in high school choir. *Bulletin of the Council for Research in Music Education, 170*, 63–77.

Clandinin, D. J. (1985). Personal practical knowledge: A study of teachers' classroom images. *Curriculum Inquiry, 15*(4), 361–385. https://doi.org/10.2307/1179683

Delpit, L. D. (1995). *Other people's children: Cultural conflict in the classroom.* New York, NY: Norton.

Erickson, F. (2005). Culture in society and in educational practices. In J. A. Banks & C. A. M. Banks (Eds.), *Multicultural education: Issues and perspectives* (5th ed., pp. 31–60). Hoboken, NJ: Wiley.

Gay, G. (2002). Preparing for culturally responsive teaching. *Journal of Teacher Education, 53*(2), 106–116.

Grant, C. A., & Ladson-Billings, G. J. (1997). *Dictionary of multicultural education.* Phoenix, AZ: Oryz Press.

Inda, J. X., & Rosaldo, R. (2002). *The anthropology of globalization: A reader.* Malden, MA: Blackwell.

Joyce, V. M. (2003). *Bodies that sing: The formation of singing subjects* (Doctoral dissertation). Retrieved from ProQuest Dissertations & Theses. (AAT NQ78458).

Karlsen, S. (2013). Immigrant students and the "homeland music": Meanings, negotiations, and implications. *Research Studies in Music Education, 35*(2), 161–177. https://doi.org/10.1177/1321103X13508057

Kelly-McHale, J. (2011). *The relationship between children's musical identities and music teacher beliefs and practices in an elementary general music classroom* (Doctoral dissertation). Retrieved from ProQuest Dissertations & Theses. (AAT 3456672).

Kelly-McHale, J. (2013). The influence of music teacher beliefs and practices on the expression of musical identity in an elementary general music classroom. *Journal of Research in Music Education, 61*(2), 195–216. https://doi.org/10.1177/0022429413485439

Ladson-Billings, G. J. (1994). *The dream-keepers: Successful teachers of African American children.* San Francisco, CA: Jossey-Bass.

Ladson-Billings, G. J. (2002). I ain't writin' nuttin': Permissions to fail and demands to succeed in urban classrooms. In L. D. Delpit & J. K. Dowdy (Eds.), *The skin that we speak: Thoughts on language and culture in the classroom* (pp. 107–120). New York, NY: Norton.

Lum, C.-H. (2007). *Musical networks of children: An ethnography of elementary school children in Singapore* (Doctoral dissertation, University of Washington). Retrieved from ProQuest Dissertations & Theses. (AAT 3265372).

Lum, C.-H., & Campbell, P. S. (2009). "El camaleon": The musical secrets of Mirella Valdez. In C. R. Abril & J. L. Kerchner (Eds.), *Musical experience in our lives: Things we learn and meanings we make* (pp. 113–126). Lanham, MD: Rowman & Littlefield.

Moll, L. C., & González, G. (2004). Engaging life: A funds-of-knowledge approach to multicultural education. In J. A. Banks & C. A. M. Banks (Eds.), *Handbook of research on multicultural education* (2nd ed., pp. 699–715). San Francisco, CA: Jossey-Bass.

Olneck, M. R. (2004). Immigrants and education in the United States. In J. A. Banks & C. A. M. Banks (Eds.), *Handbook of research on multicultural education* (2nd ed., pp. 381–403). San Francisco, CA: Jossey-Bass.

O'Toole, P. (1994). I sing in a choir, but I have no voice. *Visions of Research in Music Education, 6.* Retrieved from http://www-usr.rider.edu/~vrme/

Root, M. P. (2004). Multiracial families and children: Implications for educational research and practice. In J. A. Banks & C. A. M. Banks (Eds.), *Handbook of research on multicultural education* (2nd ed.). San Francisco, CA: Jossey-Bass.

Shaw, J. T. (2015). "Knowing their world": Urban choral music educators' knowledge of context. *Journal of Research in Music Education, 63*(2), 198–223. https://doi.org/10.1177/0022429415584377

Shaw, J. T. (2016). "The music I was meant to sing": Adolescent choral students' perceptions of culturally responsive pedagogy. *Journal of Research in Music Education*, *63*(2), 198–223.

Skerrett, A. (2008). Racializing educational change: Melting pot and mosaic influences on educational policy and practice. *Journal of Educational Change*, *9*(3), 261–280.

Suárez-Orozco, C., Suárez-Orozco, M. M., & Doucet, F. (2004). The academic engagement and achievement of Latino youth. In J. A. Banks & C. A. M. Banks (Eds.), *Handbook of research on multicultural education* (2nd ed., pp. 420–440). San Francisco, CA: Jossey-Bass.

Suárez-Orozco, C., Suárez-Orozco, M. M., & Todorova, I. (2008). *Learning a new land: Immigrant students in American society* (1st ed.). Cambridge, MA: Harvard University Press.

Villegas, A. M., & Lucas, T. (2002). Preparing culturally responsive teachers: Rethinking the curriculum. *Journal of Teacher Education*, *53*(1), 20–32. https://doi.org/10.1177/0022487102053001003

3 Culturally Responsive Teaching in the North Side Choir

The community in which the North Side Choir was situated boasted a large immigrant population, including residents from countries such as Mexico, Guatemala, the Philippines, India, Cambodia, Somalia, Romania, Sweden, Pakistan, Iraq, Iran, and Lebanon. Students attending the neighborhood's public schools spoke over 40 languages, evidencing the cultural diversity present in the community. The university at which the choir rehearsed contributed a college-town atmosphere to the neighborhood.

A distinguishing feature of the community's demography was its sizeable Korean population. Signs for the neighborhood's expressway exit read "Koreatown," and street signs designated one of its major thoroughfares "honorary Seoul Drive." The community was home to Korean businesses, restaurants, churches, and retirement centers. It featured two Korean-language newspapers, a Korean television station, and a Korean radio station.

During the choir's registration process, North Side singers identified as African American (6%), Asian American (30%), Latino (23%), and White/European (41%). During one of my visits, students described their cultural identities during an icebreaker activity. Their responses offered a more nuanced picture of cultural diversity present in the choir than did the choir's registration categories. Students shared that they identified as German, French, Asian, Mexican, Filipino, Western European, African American, Australian, Dutch, Korean, Irish, Puerto Rican, Polish, Brazilian, Chinese, Ukrainian, Russian, and Assyrian. Several students also mentioned that they were multiracial or multiethnic. Of the three choirs, the North Side Choir was the most socioeconomically diverse, with families distributed relatively evenly throughout the organization's family income categories (see Table 1.3).

Teacher's Biographical Sketch

Ms. Lisa Rose was born to Korean immigrants in the very neighborhood in which she conducted the North Side Choir. She related:

> My parents were music educators in Korea, but when they came here, my dad worked in a convenience store. So, we were poor. . . . My

mom is one of five girls in her family . . . when she moved here, they lived in a one-bedroom apartment with my grandparents and aunts all together . . . eventually everyone got their own apartment in the same complex. My dad started his own business and then moved to the 'burbs, worked extremely hard, and created a great life for us.

The apartment complex in which Ms. Rose lived with her recently-immigrated extended family was situated within the city's Koreatown, a then thriving ethnic enclave. She described her childhood experiences as having been thoroughly infused with elements of Korean culture:

My parents never spoke in English to me. A lot of my friends who were born in America spoke English with their parents too, but I didn't know how to speak English until I was five. . . . I only ate Korean food. All my bedtime stories were in Korean. Everything was Korean, so I might as well just have been living in Korea.

Ms. Rose held a Bachelor of Arts as well as a Master of Music, with dual emphases in performance and music education. Her parents, both of whom were musicians, provided a music-filled home environment that inspired her to become a music educator. She began studying piano at age four, and considered her involvement with a Korean youth chorus to be a formative musical experience. There, she sang under a Korean American conductor who served as an influential professional role model. It was this ensemble Ms. Rose identified as representing an ideal vocal model for her students, and she provided a recording for discussion. While the recording exemplified the Western classical style of singing, she emphasized that this was only one of many possible ideal sounds for her students:

This is my ideal children's choir sound, but at the same time, I wouldn't want my kids to sing "*Siyahamba*" like that. Especially since we're always singing different world music, it's very important to be able to change your tone and vocal technique, so this is just one way I want my children's choir to sound.

Elements of Ms. Rose's Culturally Responsive Practice

As a fourth-year teacher, Ms. Rose considered herself to be in the early stages of implementing premises of CRT. The following field note excerpt describes a typical North Side rehearsal:

The university chapel in which the choir rehearsed featured hardwood floors, high ceilings, and wooden chairs arranged in pew-like rows. Ms. Rose taught students from her position at a grand piano on stage at the front of the room. She had arranged for her Prelude and Lyric choirs' rehearsals to overlap by thirty minutes to facilitate joint rehearsals. Lyric singers efficiently took their places in the third and fourth rows behind Prelude singers already seated in the front two rows. During this transition, the ensembles sang Praetorius's *"Jubilate Deo,"* a piece students considered one of the choir's "greatest hits." Their sound was characteristic of the Western European tradition of choral singing, featuring tall, unified vowels; a carefully blended sound; extensive use of head voice; and a focused, ringing quality to the tone.

Ms. Rose had established a routine of using this combined rehearsal time for music theory and sight-singing instruction. She led students in singing a major scale on solfège syllables, followed by an interval drill. Students sang, "do to re is a major second, do to mi is a major third," and so on, identifying each interval of the major scale. As they sang, Ms. Rose pointed to a small white board on which she had visually represented the scale as eight dots in a diagonal arrangement, each labeled with solfège syllables and scale degree numbers. When she suggested, "Let's do it in a round!" the children playfully groaned before performing the exercise in two parts. She offered feedback on their "overly bright" tone, encouraging them to sing with tall vowels.

Ms. Rose dismissed the Prelude choir, and Lyric students proceeded with their routine choral warm-ups. Their exercises focused on elements of *bel canto* technique: posture, breathing, vowel unification, resonance, range extension, and diction. They concluded with a comical round about having tea with a Duchess, but the humor seemed lost on the singers, who focused intently on achieving the tone their teacher requested without cracking a smile. Aside from students' singing, one could hear a pin drop in the highly structured classroom environment.

When Ms. Rose announced the next song, *"Lizela,"* a *Xhosa* folk song from South Africa, the students reacted enthusiastically. She taught the piece orally, having been informed by a colleague who had traveled to South Africa to research the music that this was how the piece would be learned in its culture of origin. When the students could accurately sing in three-part harmony with appropriate vocal timbre and style, they learned the movements with which the song was traditionally performed. Throughout the process, the choir referenced a field recording made by Ms. Rose's colleague, which featured South African musicians performing the piece.

The next piece was a gospel standard, "I Need You to Survive." When Ms. Rose began to play the piano introduction, the students exclaimed, "Yes!" After listening to one verse, she asked students to sing in a style that was "really soulful." They responded by singing in their chest voices with a darker, more soulful sound, but Ms. Rose noted that not all of the pitches were accurate. She reacted by saying, "Whoa! Did that sound good?" One student responded, "no," and others appeared frozen. They sang again, more cautiously, and with careful attention to singing the correct pitches. Noticing that the students had "lost their soulfulness" while focusing on pitch accuracy, she modeled the desired sound for them with a powerful, well-developed chest voice.

Ms. Rose worked with students to add dynamic nuance to their delivery of the text. She guided them to notice that some of the lyrics repeated three times, asking students what purpose the repetition served. Together, they decided that repeating these words should have the effect of intensifying the message conveyed through the lyrics. She invited singers to push and pull with their hands to feel the tension and release in each phrase, noting, "You can use your hands to show what you're feeling." Students did as she suggested, resulting in some of the most facially and musically expressive singing to occur yet.

The following section describes elements of Ms. Rose's pedagogy in relation to Gay's (2002) essential elements of CRT. As this chapter will illustrate, some aspects of her instruction aligned with tenets of CRT, while others were more suggestive of a Eurocentric approach to choral music education.

Developing a Knowledge Base About Cultural Diversity

Ms. Rose's personal practical knowledge as a second-generation immigrant proved advantageous in designing CRT for her substantial population of immigrant students. She noted:

> Because my childhood was similar to theirs, I have an advantage in that I can connect with them that way. I came from this neighborhood . . . naturally you're gonna understand them more, because I'm assuming I lived a similar day-to-day lifestyle. So if you haven't, then you don't really know what they're going through.

As a result of her family's experiences, she understood challenges involved in the process of acculturation, including linguistic barriers, family separations and reunifications, and cultural disorientation. She noted, "I might be more sensitive to it because I went through the same thing. Or more aware of it than somebody that didn't have that experience, culturally."

During a previous research collaboration exploring Ms. Rose's work with a predominantly Mexican American community (Shaw, 2015), she described her awareness of factors affecting parent-teacher communication:

> I grew up with my mom being afraid to speak to teachers, so she was never really involved. She knows how to speak English and she's good at it, but it scares her to death. I don't know why. So I can connect with their parents in that way.

(p. 208)

Ms. Rose was alert to the possibility that linguistic differences could make some parents hesitant to communicate with teachers. Research has also suggested that immigrant parents may be hesitant to interact with school officials due to anxiety about immigration policy (Suárez-Orozco & Suárez-Orozco, 2001; Valdés, 1996) or may maintain distance from teachers as a sign of professional respect (Lopez, 2001). Potential exists for teachers to misinterpret dynamics such as these as a lack of parental investment in their children's education.

To the contrary, Ms. Rose's awareness of these factors enabled her to work effectively with families who had differing approaches to parent-teacher relationships. Recognizing that due to factors such as linguistic barriers and immigration status, some parents trusted oral communication over written correspondence and felt more comfortable communicating with other parents than with the organization's staff, she established a choir parent network. Parent liaisons communicated important logistical details with families, fielded questions at parent meetings, and encouraged new families to join the choir. The parent network served as an invaluable resource through which Ms. Rose developed knowledge about families' cultural backgrounds, musical experiences, and orientations toward music education.

Designing Culturally Relevant Curricula

Ms. Rose's efforts to practice CRT focused primarily on Gay's (2002) second component, which encompasses incorporating diverse content and perspectives into curricula. She was enthusiastic about teaching repertoire that represented diverse cultural traditions and strived to present it in a culturally valid manner. As this chapter will illuminate, her curricular decision-making was driven more by her desire for students to experience repertoire representing diverse cultural traditions than by considerations of particular students' cultural backgrounds, an approach that only partially addresses the goals of CRT. Additionally, Ms. Rose's approach to content integration resembled what Banks (2005) termed an "additive approach," in which diverse content and perspectives function as appendages to a curriculum that remains Eurocentric at its core. This approach presented some limitations on students' perceptions of cultural responsiveness, as singers' portraits will illustrate.

Cultural Congruity in Instruction

Even when a diverse range of musical genres gain entrance into the curriculum, teachers may continue to approach them through the pedagogical lens of Western classical music. As a result, students may experience discontinuities between the ways they experience music inside and outside of the music classroom. In contrast, Ms. Rose's pedagogical approach included varied terms of engagement (e.g., vocal timbres, vocal styles, aural vs. notated learning strategies), depending on the cultural context of the music studied. As exemplified in the previous field note excerpt, she taught orally or from notation depending on how each selection would be taught in its culture of origin. She researched and taught students to sing with the vocal tone, timbre, and style appropriate to each selection's culture of origin. Recognizing the centrality of physical movement to musical experience in many of the world's cultures, she frequently used carefully researched movement as a means of enhancing the cultural validity of the choir's performances. The diversity of learning experiences Ms. Rose provided opened avenues for students to engage with music in culturally preferred ways and build upon cultural assets they brought to the classroom, thus promoting cultural congruity. The following are portraits of three singers whose experiences shed light on CRT as practiced in the North Side Choir.

Sarah: "I Want to Sound More Classical"

Sarah, a 12-year-old third-year member of the choir, had studied violin for five years and piano for two, but discontinued piano because "it cluttered up her schedule with all the activities she had picked up." One of her favorite activities was dance, and her instinctive response to hearing music was to mentally choreograph dances. Her interest in dance wove its way into our discussions of her music listening preferences, which encompassed country, pop, and "barre music," meaning "what you listen to at the ballet barre." A self-described perfectionist, she related, "I like things being right the first time. I can be very critical of myself and will be open with my criticism if the [choir] doesn't sound good."

Sarah described her family as "prioritizing academics," "focused on getting things done," and "in a word, supportive." Choral singing was an interest shared by her mother and brother, who also sang in the North Side Choir. Sarah described her household as "musical":

> If I start singing, my mom might just make up a harmony. She helps me out with my violin. We have a piano at home that we sometimes play. My brother plays the drums, too. We have a lot of instruments around the house.

She described her father, a professor, as being "more academic" than musical, and dismissed any music making she did with friends as being "not serious."

Born to Korean immigrants, Sarah self-identified as "Korean or Korean American." Her parents immigrated to the United States at ages five and eight and attended American public schools. She explained, "They were both born in Korea, but moved here at a really young age. So, if you talk to them, you would probably think they were born here." She further noted, "My parents both speak Korean, but I never learned how to speak Korean. We never really spoke it around the house." When I asked Sarah whether she believed it was important to identify herself as Korean or Korean American, she replied:

> Yes, being Korean is an important part of who I am and if I don't know that, it's a serious problem. It doesn't 100% define me, but defines a huge portion of me: what I am, and who I am.

Sarah's definitions of "musician" and "singer" emphasized a command of music theory, an ability to engage with music creatively, technical proficiency, and devoting a significant amount of time to one's craft. She asserted:

> A real singer should be good at music and singing and if they have raw talent, should keep working to improve it . . . they should know theory and be able to compose their own songs. Or, just be like the opera singer where she can reach high notes and probably spends a lot of time working on music and [believes] music is really important.

She stopped short of considering herself a musician, explaining, "music isn't the number one thing in my life." Yet she did consider herself and all the members of the North Side Choir to be singers because "it's what we do. We go twice a week and work on it [singing]. We know our theory and fulfill most aspects of [being] a singer." Reiterating the importance of knowing music theory, she stressed, "it's one of the basic foundations of being a singer."

Sarah identified Ms. Mary Ann, a classically trained opera singer who had performed for the choir, as a vocal model she most desired to emulate. Specifically, she admired Mary Ann's extensive range, technical proficiency, agility, and ability to seamlessly shift between vocal registers. Having selected a Western classical vocal model as her own ideal, Sarah reacted positively to Ms. Rose's chosen vocal model. She stated that she would like to sound like the Korean Children's Choir because "They sound like a big choir of Miss Mary Ann's." When I asked if the singers in the recording would fit in well as members of the North Side Choir, she answered, "It depends on how well that choir would be able to adjust to different styles of music," referencing the stylistic versatility her teacher valued.

As the following exchange demonstrates, Ms. Rose drew upon personal practical knowledge as a second-generation Korean American to design learning experiences Sarah perceived to be responsive to her cultural identity:

Sarah: We do a lot of Korean songs. . . . We did one called *"Arirang"*. . . .
         Since Ms. Rose is also Korean, she's able to help us with pronunciation, which is good because I actually don't speak Korean. She helps us understand it too, so when we sing Korean songs, we know what we're singing. It's not just a bunch of words in a different language, we're able to connect with the song more.

Julia: In what ways does she help you understand it?

Sarah: Well, first she'll give us the direct translation into English and then she'll do, like, the meaning it has to people who sing it. So that way we know the importance it has to people, so we can convey that when we sing.

Julia: So, for example, tell me a little bit about *"Arirang."*

Sarah: Well, she told us it's a folk song about someone wandering alone, so we sing it according to the theme it has . . . and the tone, we sing it more folk-y.

Julia: What is it like to sing in that folk style?

Sarah: *"Arirang"* is actually one of the only pieces in Korean that I've ever known. I knew it when I was really little and I would sing it a lot. I never really knew what it meant, but I would just sing it the way I heard it. It came with a little bit of a folkish twang when my mom or grandpa sang it, so that [twang] was already there.

As a U.S.-born daughter of Korean immigrants, Sarah's identity encompassed connections to both Korean and American culture. Her experience singing *"Arirang"* was meaningful to her in that it fostered a sense of connection to her parental culture of origin. She received her teacher's repertoire choice as culturally relevant, having known the song since she was a young child and sung it with family members. Rather than insinuating that the "folkish twang" with which her mother and grandfather sang was incorrect, Ms. Rose provided an opportunity to cultivate that tone within a culturally appropriate context. Sarah observed that the vocal tone and style required to perform the piece were "already there," within her range of capabilities, having previously sung the song with family members. Therefore, singing *"Arirang"* opened avenues for Sarah to capitalize on prior knowledge, previous experiences, and culturally informed performance practices, resulting in an experience of cultural congruity.

Ms. Rose was also able to deepen and extend Sarah's understanding of *"Arirang,"* as evidenced by Sarah's observation that she never fully understood the song's meaning until she sang it with the choir. She appreciated the opportunity to sing in Korean because although her parents spoke Korean, she never learned the language herself. Singing *"Arirang"* thus promoted Sarah's cultural competence, helping to deepen her knowledge of her own cultural heritage. She emphasized that such opportunities are "important because it's another place to learn about ourselves and our backgrounds. The songs give us a connection to our backgrounds or our ethnicity."

Ms. Rose's and Sarah's cultural backgrounds shared important commonalities, providing potentially fertile ground for CRT. Both were second-generation Korean Americans and spent their childhoods in the same neighborhood, which boasted a thriving Korean community. Drawing upon personal practical knowledge, Ms. Rose provided some experiences with Korean music that Sarah considered culturally responsive. However, as the following conversation demonstrates, even a teacher whose cultural background corresponds closely with that of her students cannot safely make assumptions about the learning experiences they will consider relevant:

Julia: Some music teachers would say, "Oh, a Korean song. Sarah's Korean. It's going to be easy for her," but that's not necessarily right?

Sarah: Mm hmm. Ms. Rose actually thought that I spoke Korean and I was just a normal Korean kid who likes spicy food, which is kind of the opposite. I really can't stand spicy food because it burns my tongue and I don't really know any Korean except for that one song.

Sarah's observations illustrate the importance of taking individual variability among members of any cultural group into account when designing culturally responsive instruction. As she explained, although she identifies with Korean culture, her teacher cannot assume that she is "a normal Korean kid," that she speaks Korean fluently, or that she will consider Korean folk songs to be culturally relevant. Her comments imply that misguided teacher assumptions about students' cultural identities can thwart their well-intentioned efforts to practice CRT, even when teachers' and students' cultural backgrounds share commonalities.

Delores: "When You Look at Me, You Can Kind of Tell"

Delores, a twelve-year-old seventh grader, was a fourth-year veteran member of the choir. Her dark purple glasses and serious facial expressions gave her an intellectual appearance during rehearsals. She was born and raised in the same U.S. city in which she resided. When asked to describe her cultural identity, she chose the descriptor "biracial," referencing her parents' cultural identities:

Delores: I am African American and German and that's it, because my dad is German and my mom is African American.

Julia: Do you think it's important to identify yourself as German or African American?

Delores: Not really, because when you look at me, you can kind of tell.

Julia: Do you think there's more to being German or African-American than how somebody looks?

Delores: Well, the only reason you can tell by just looking at me is I'm not dark enough to be all African American. So, you know there's something else in me besides just that.

I think they'd know, "Oh, she's African American and something else."

Julia: Is it important to you that people know what the "something else" is?

Delores: Um, [it's] more a private thing. They just don't need to know . . . a lot of people at school, they'll walk up to me and say, "Is one

of your parents Black and the other White?" Or they ask if I'm
Hispanic, 'cause a lot of people don't understand. They're just like,
"What?" I've been asked so many times, I don't even really notice
it anymore.

For Delores, part of the process of adolescent self-discovery involved making
sense of her biracial identity. Family influences and peer interaction were salient
screening lenses through which she viewed her emerging sense of self (see Root,
2004). Phenotype was also a significant experiential component of biracial
identity for Delores, as she fielded questions from peers attempting to make
sense of her appearance so frequently that she "didn't even notice it anymore."

Delores clarified that her father was born in the U.S., but studied abroad:
"He lived there [in Germany] for all of college and then a little bit after that.
Then he came back and found my mom. My mom lived in Pittsburgh. . . .
Some of my family is also from Nashville." When asked how she might rep-
resent her cultural background in a school project, she responded:

I don't know! Pittsburgh isn't really famous for anything, but . . . you
know how it's really hilly there? They have these cars on the side of hills
so you can go up and down the hills. I guess I'd bring a little model of
that because that's the first thing I see whenever I go there. Then for
Germany, I guess I'd just bring a flag. For Nashville, Tennessee, I don't
know what I'd bring.

Throughout our interviews, Delores described her cultural identity in relation to specific locations that held significance to her family: Nashville, Tennessee; Pittsburgh, Pennsylvania; and Germany. For instance, she described her
father as "German" rather than "Caucasian" or "American," even though he
was born and spent the majority of his life in the United States. Searching for
a word to describe her Caucasian parentage, she attached the label "German"
to her own identity as well. This was interesting considering that she was
not born in, has never resided in, and has never visited Germany herself. She
considered her racial and ethnic identity to be "more of a private thing," and
resisted labels or categorization that others seemed eager to impose upon her.

Delores's primary musical involvement had been through the children's
choir, an experience she perceived to be centered upon the Western classical
canon. She noted, "since we sing classical so much, I just like to hear something else different." She did not aspire to sound like Ms. Rose's classically
oriented vocal model, but remarked that those voices would fit well within the
North Side Choir "because of how much classical they sing." Her definition
of musician emphasized "knowing one's instrument" and fluency with solfège:

You have to know what you're doing. . . . Like, if you are a pianist, then
you have to know what the keys are or if you're a singer, then you should
really know the solfège. . . . You should know your instrument.

Although she had five years of choral experience, she only considered herself a musician "in some ways." She devalued her ability to learn music aurally, and didn't consider herself "a true musician" because of a perceived lack of fluency with solfège: "I know how to sing by ear, but I don't really know the solfège. If I knew the solfège, then I'd consider myself a true musician."

When asked why she chose to continue her membership in choir year after year, Delores replied, "It's just so much fun to be able to sing and learn about different cultures." While she valued learning about previously unfamiliar cultures in choir, she did not perceive Ms. Rose's instruction to be responsive to her own cultural background or identity. The following exchange is representative of our conversations:

Julia: Do you identify with any choir songs in terms of your own cultural background?
Delores: No, not really.
Julia: Not at all?
Delores: [Negatively] Mm.
Julia: Which one might have come closest, or were they all equally unrelated to your background?
Delores: They were all just equally not.

The curriculum Delores experienced served to broaden her cultural horizons rather than to prompt learning about her own cultural identity or heritage. As she made sense of her biracial identity, she did not find her musical experiences in choir relevant to her process of self-discovery. While researchers have noted that after-school activities can serve as sites for adolescents' identity construction, opening possibilities for them to explore various facets of their cultural identities (Root, 2004; Suárez-Orozco, Suárez-Orozco, & Doucet, 2004), the potential for the North Side Choir to serve as one such site for Delores remained unexplored.

That Delores's classroom experiences did not result in instruction she considered culturally responsive may relate to aspects of the North Side's learning environment that contradicted premises of CRT, which are discussed subsequently. Nevertheless, her experiences suggest some implications for teachers:

- That the parents of students who identify as bi- or multiracial may not be bi- or multiracial themselves merits consideration and suggests implications such as the following:

  - Conversations taking placing in the home may help students to make sense of their identities and experiences, but teachers cannot *assume* that such conversations routinely take place. Classroom activities prompting students to reflect on aspects of their cultural identities may compliment dialogue occurring at home, or may be among the first times students have engaged substantively with these topics. Teachers will therefore need to respond to individuals' varying degrees of comfort and facility with these topics.

- Students who identify as bi- or multiracial may value teachers' efforts to represent contributions of musicians who also identify as bi- or multiracial in both the official and the symbolic curriculum.

- As Delores's experience exemplified, bi- or multiracial students may constantly field inquiries from peers about their cultural identities, not all of which may be respectful encounters. Teachers might then guard against putting such students on the spot with requests to publicly describe their cultural identities or serve as culture bearers.
- Classroom projects exploring identity, autobiographical assignments, or inquiries into the musical experiences students would consider culturally relevant may be welcomed as opportunities for students to explore facets of their identities or may result in awkward, socially compromising, or confusing experiences. Considering this, teachers might offer projects aimed at developing cultural competence as one possibility from a menu of options, affording students genuine choice about whether and how to participate.
- Assignments with response formats affording confidentiality, such as journaling, may be appealing to students who desire for aspects of their cultural identities to remain "more of a private thing."
- Creative engagements, such as musical composition, might open attractive possibilities for CRT in that students can control which facets of their cultural identities to express artistically and in what manner, a broadly applicable implication that is discussed further in Chapter 6.

Daniella: "I Can't Really Go a Day Without Singing"

Daniella, a twelve-year-old seventh grader and fifth-year member of the choir, described herself as "complicated," "unexpected," and "funny." As she explained, self-expression through music had been a routine aspect of her life since early childhood: "Ever since I was little, I was always singing. There's videos of me and my sister standing on the stairs singing songs with microphones made out of toilet paper rolls." She studied piano and was an active member of three choirs: the North Side Choir, her church's youth choir, and her school's choir, which her father conducted. Members of her extended family were musically inclined, and she described elaborate performances her family had staged and sing-alongs with aunts, uncles, and cousins gathered around the piano. She identified one of her cousins as the vocal model she most desired to emulate.

Like the other two student participants at this site, Daniella's definition of "musician" emphasized notational fluency: "What makes someone a musician is if they do something where it involves sheet music . . . like someone who would play an instrument or a singer." She unquestionably identified as a musician and singer, relating:

> I'm in three different choirs, so I'm a musician. . . . I can't really go a day without singing. I do it all the time, and it sometimes gets annoying to my friends. . . . It makes me feel happier and more confident in myself.

She reacted positively to Ms. Rose's preferred vocal model, explaining, "I'm fine with learning how to sing in any style because the more variety of styles you have, the better you can become and the more skilled you can be." She was confident that any singer could learn to style shift: "if singers have the perseverance and dedication to sing in a certain style that they're not used to, then if they practice a lot, they can probably end up getting that style."

Born in the same U.S. city in which she lived, Daniella self-identified as "Puerto Rican and Mexican." Her father was born in the United States to Puerto Rican migrants, and delighted in sharing Puerto Rican culture with Daniella. She explained that visits with extended family residing in Puerto Rico helped her maintain a connection with her heritage. Daniella's maternal grandparents immigrated to the United States from Mexico, but her extended family no longer resided in Mexico and opportunities to visit had been limited. As a result, she felt more loosely connected to Mexican culture.

Several generations removed from her grandparents' and great-grandparents' transitions to the United States, Daniella considered her parental cultures of origin more distantly related to her daily experiences. She did not speak Spanish. If given the opportunity to present about her cultural heritage at school, she would prepare by turning to the internet rather than family members' or her own experiences. At first, she did not feel that music related to her cultural background, stating:

> I don't really know songs in Spanish. I don't know any Hispanic or Puerto Rican songs.
> I don't really know Mexican music. I probably do, but don't realize that it's Mexican music. . . . I'm not singing a lot of Mexican songs. I never really listen to them.

While Daniella had yet to have an experience in choir that related to her Mexican heritage, she described occasions on which she sang music relevant to her Puerto Rican background:

Daniella: We did a Puerto Rican song last year and my sister, in Prelude, they did two. On my dad's side, my *Titi* Lucia knew the songs we were doing because they were traditional Puerto Rican songs.
Julia: What were you singing?
Daniella: "*En Mi Viejo San Juan.*" She and my dad were singing along, because I guess my *abuela* made them learn it. My dad's other

sisters and brothers, they knew it too, so my mom took a video and tried sending it to them and put it on Facebook too.

Julia: How did people respond to that song?

Daniella: A lot of people in the audience liked it. There were some Puerto Ricans who knew the song, so I saw them singing along. They were just brought to tears because it's almost like their national anthem. I forgot what the words mean. . . . I think it mostly has to do with Puerto Rico. That's all I really know about it.

Julia: How did it make you feel to perform that piece?

Daniella: When I found out that it was in Spanish, my first thought was, "my dad might know this song." So, when I got home, I asked and he knew the song. He told me that if we performed it, he was going to invite my *Titi* Lucia so she could hear it because it's her favorite song.

Daniella described her performance of "*En Mi Viejo San Juan*" as one of her most meaningful performances as a choir member. She fondly recalled the warm reception she received from family members backstage after the performance. Her father and aunts had been moved to tears by her performance and expressed how proud they were of her.

Ms. Rose recalled Daniella's family approaching her after the concert, but attached this memory to a Brazilian selection rather than to "*En Mi Viejo San Juan.*"

Ms. Rose: We did a Brazilian piece last year and I didn't realize how many Brazilian students I had and their parents absolutely loved it. I wasn't really thinking about trying to please those students. I was just choosing a piece and I realized that it really does make a difference to try to do as many different cultures as possible.

Julia: So how did you choose that piece?

Ms. Rose: Oh, I just . . . J. W. Pepper really liked it, so . . .

Julia: Then it just so happened that you had some Brazilian students?

Ms. Rose: Yeah. I thought they were just Hispanic, but I didn't realize they were Brazilian specifically. I had no idea. But we had, I think two separate families, and they came up to me and thanked me for putting it on the program and they loved it. . . . [Daniella's father] said his mother sang it to him all the time. . . . I had no idea. It was kind of cool.

That Ms. Rose remained unaware of Daniella's specific connection to "*En Mi Viejo San Juan*" suggests that the culturally responsive nature of this experience was more serendipitous than intentional. She explained that her repertoire selection process was motivated by a desire to present a variety of culturally diverse music rather than responding to particular students' cultural backgrounds or identities (she had "no idea" about students' connections to Puerto Rican or Brazilian culture). Her comment that she "thought students were just Hispanic" reveals essentialist thinking in that she regarded her Hispanic students as one homogeneous group, rather than intentionally responding to individuals' specific cultural identities.

Interestingly, this repertoire choice unintentionally created possibilities for Daniella to explore her Puerto Rican heritage, resulting in an experience she perceived to be culturally responsive. She summarized the importance of learning music representative of her own cultural background:

> It helps you know more about your culture. It makes you feel more confident as a singer cause it's like, "oh, that song is from my culture" and then you want to sing it good. You want to please your parents or other people you know from that culture, or . . . it might be rare for you to like sing in that language, so you wanna do good on it cause it's the first time that you've done it. So, you wanna make sure it's like, "Oh, this is a song to remember."

Both Mateo and Daniella perceived their experiences singing *"En Mi Viejo San Juan"* as being responsive to their cultural background, enabling an illuminating comparison. Of the participants in this study, Mateo and Daniella were the fewest and greatest number of generations removed from their family's transitions to the (contiguous) United States, respectively. Mateo, a first-generation migrant, had experienced the sense of longing described in the song firsthand. Two years after performing *"En Mi Viejo San Juan,"* he was able to articulate the song's meaning and describe the significance it held for him personally. Daniella also considered the piece "a song to remember." However, a year after her performance, she could not recall it's meaning, vaguely summarizing, "it's mostly about Puerto Ricans."

Learning experiences based on *"En Mi Viejo San Juan"* developed both singers' cultural competence, but in different ways. For Mateo, the piece provided an opportunity to sing in his first language, spoke directly to his lived experiences, and affirmed his clearly defined sense of Puerto Rican identity. For Daniella, the piece presented a "rare" opportunity to sing in Spanish, to learn about her cultural heritage, and to explore a comparatively lesser-known facet of her cultural identity. Their experiences illuminate ways in which migrant and immigrant students' experiences might differ according to generation.

Daniella's experiences challenge the notion that "homeland music," or folk music associated with students' parental culture(s) of origin, will automatically resonate with students (Karlsen, 2013). Students may in fact enjoy learning those traditions, but the experiences may present new learning or offer a productive challenge as opposed to automatically resonating as validating or affirming. Additionally, second- and subsequent generation (im)migrant students featured in this book felt connected to both their parental culture(s) of origin and adolescent mainstream culture. This suggests that age is an important facet of cultural identity to consider when planning learning experiences, and that "youth culture" is one of the possible cultures to which CRT might respond.

An important dimension of learning "*En Mi Viejo San Juan*" for Daniella was the way the piece catalyzed interactions within her family. Whenever Ms. Rose introduced a piece sung in Spanish, Daniella's first thought was "I wonder if my Dad knows this," and she couldn't wait to take it home to discuss with him. Extended family members attended Daniella's concert specifically to hear "*En Mi Viejo San Juan*," and she beamed as she described their positive reception of her performance. Her mother emailed videos of her performance and shared them via social media, allowing geographically distant family to experience the concert virtually. Thus, Daniella's experience with "*En Mi Viejo San Juan*" bridged her experiences at home and in choir, fostering meaningful connections with her family.

Tensions With CRT

From North Side students' descriptions of their experiences, four themes emerged that were in tension with the theory of CRT: an additive approach to curriculum design, content integration without a student-centered orientation, a score-centered learning environment, and perceived value hierarchies that privileged the Western classical style of singing.

Additive Approach

Despite the diversity of cultural and musical traditions Ms. Rose presented for classroom exploration, students perceived the central focus of the curriculum to be the Western classical tradition. This perception was evidenced by student remarks such as "we sing classical so much," "all of our hits are classical," and "we're just so set in the classical mode." Ms. Rose's approach to integrating diverse content resembled Banks' (2005) "additive approach," in which ethnic content and perspectives function as appendages to, rather than core components of, the curriculum (p. 246).

A unit of study leading up to the choir's December performance exemplified this additive approach. The choir was invited to appear at a university's annual Lessons and Carols program, a service of Christian worship incorporating music and biblical readings. For this occasion, Ms. Rose selected repertoire that primarily corresponded to the Western classical tradition. Students additionally collaborated with the university's gospel choir to perform "Jesus, Oh What a Wonderful Child." Students perceived the single gospel selection to be an "add-on" to the classical repertoire that comprised the core of the concert program. Preparations for this concert, which were dominated by Eurocentric discourse norms, consumed most of the choir's time during the fall semester.

Content Integration Lacking a Student-Centered Orientation

As Ms. Rose explained, her curricular decisions were guided by a desire for students to encounter a diverse array of cultural traditions more than they were motivated by an interest in responding to the cultural backgrounds of particular students. The following excerpt is representative of our conversations:

Ms. Rose: Well, for North Side, I don't really focus on their cultural backgrounds because it's so diverse that I just try to do a general mixed cultural program. I don't really look at them [students]. I try to pick pieces as diverse as I can, but mostly look at the music itself to see if it's appropriate for them.

Julia: Okay. So you will not necessarily choose music to reflect the specific learners in your choir?

Ms. Rose: Right. I'll choose a program and try to make it multicultural as well as have it fit their level musically.

Julia: How about your interactions with students? Are you thinking about their cultural backgrounds at all?

Ms. Rose: I probably do subconsciously, but I don't know that I'm doing that actively.

While students perceived some of their experiences to be culturally responsive, connections between students' musical and cultural identities happened serendipitously; often by accident rather than by design.

A common misconception among choral educators may be that singing repertoire representing diverse cultural traditions in and of itself constitutes CRT. However, student-centeredness is a distinguishing feature of this approach to pedagogy. Performing repertoire representative of diverse cultural traditions, while itself a worthy goal, may fall short of cultural responsiveness when no attempt is made to align repertoire choices with the knowledge, strengths, experiences, perspectives, and learning needs of particular students. Further, diversifying repertoire only partially accomplishes the goal of designing culturally relevant curricula, which is in turn just one of many elements of CRT described by leading theorists. Limitations presented by approaching CRT primarily through performing culturally diverse repertoire are explored further in Chapter 5.

Score-Centered Rehearsal Environment

Conversations with singers and rehearsal observations revealed the score-centered (Thibeault, 2009) orientation of the North Side's learning environment. Developing students' notational fluency was a central aim of Ms. Rose's instruction and a predominant discourse norm in her rehearsal environment. That she had a routinely scheduled, designated time for working on music theory and sight-singing signaled its importance to students. She typically devoted at least one-third of available instructional time to sight-singing, practicing solfège exercises, and completing written theory assignments. Although Ms. Rose frequently taught orally when appropriate given the cultural context, singers' comments frequently devalued aural learning. For example, Delores considered reading music to be the only way to learn a song "properly."

Notational fluency was such a pervasive discourse norm in the North Side Choir's environment that it figured prominently in students' definitions of musician and singer. "Knowing theory" was central to Sarah's definitions of both "musician" and "singer." The first thought that occurred to Daniella when asked to define "musician," was "if they do something where it involves sheet music." Delores's belief that a musician is someone who can read music prevented her from considering herself a musician, despite five years of experience with the choir. Thus, the score-centeredness of the North Side's rehearsal environment influenced the ways students viewed themselves as singers and musicians, alienating some students from the belief that they were "musicians."

Perceived Value Hierarchies Concerning Vocal Timbre and Style

Ms. Rose's students exhibited openness toward a variety of vocal timbres and styles and an ability to shift fluidly between them. For example, they described the style shift required to perform the gospel piece "Jesus, Oh What a Wonderful Child":

Julia: What do you think about "Jesus, Oh What a Wonderful Child?"
Sarah: It takes a lot of effort to deliver it properly, I think.
Delores: Yeah, I think it's because we're just more used to classical than this.
Sarah: Yeah.
Julia: Is that because you've sung more classical music?
Delores: Yeah, and a lot of our hits are classical.
Julia: Okay. So you said it takes a lot of effort to deliver it properly?
Delores: Yes.
Julia: What are some things that go into singing gospel correctly?
Delores: A lot of projection and chest voice. A lot of moving and being into the music.
Julia: Is there anything special you have to do with the vocal style?
Daniella: Sometimes you have to, like, slide, but you can't do it too much. . . . You'll take out some of the letters.

Singers' comments reflected their developing awareness of performance practices appropriate for singing gospel: stylistic elements such as sliding between and bending pitches, moving expressively while singing, and singing with a different style of diction than that featured in classical music ("taking out some of the letters" rather than crisply articulating consonants). However, their remarks that "we're just more used to classical," "a lot of our hits are classical," and "we're just so set in the classical mode" reflected the centrality of the Western classical canon in the curriculum.

Despite singers' openness toward diverse cultural traditions, musical genres, and styles of singing, interview conversations suggested that students perceived a value hierarchy that positioned Western classical music as the gold standard of choral excellence. As one representative example, Sarah discussed discomfort with some of the style shifting Ms. Rose encouraged:

> In choir, I like when we do classical pieces because I feel like we excel at that. When we do pop, it does not sound as polished or our tone kind of drops. Then, when we do something more soulful, if not all of us have a soulful tone, it kind of sounds bad. Not all of us can achieve that soulfulness, so classical is something more safe and sounds better when it's performed . . . when we do pop songs, everyone gets into the song, but I feel like they sacrifice their tone. . . . [When we sing classical music,] we focus more on getting everything right and being a complete package, performance-ready.

Her comments positioned classical music as "safe," "sounding better," "getting everything right" and as a genre in which the choir "excelled." Conversely, when the choir performed genres such as pop or gospel, Sarah perceived their performances as "not sounding polished" and as "sacrificing their tone." Student commentary such as this frequently positioned Western classical singing as a "correct" way to sing while devaluing additional genres in comparison.

As one result of an additive approach to curriculum integration, which centered the Western classical canon, students amassed the most experience singing classical music. This may, in turn, have contributed to their perceptions that they "excelled" in that genre. Sarah seemed to attribute her feelings of being "like a complete package, performance-ready" to supposed inherent "goodness" of classical music, rather than to experience she had accrued in that genre. Sarah's supposition that "not all of us can achieve soulfulness" suggests a fixed rather than growth mindset toward approximating vocal timbres with which she was less experienced (Dweck, 2006). This further implies that self-efficacy may be an important determinant of singers' willingness to cross culturally informed style parameters.

Although Ms. Rose stated that she did not espouse or explicitly articulate beliefs about the superiority of Western classical music, the predominance of discourse norms associated with classical singing appeared to contribute toward students' perceptions that Western classical music was the most legitimate to study and perform. This pattern of findings parallels Rohan's (2011) discovery that high school students viewed school music education as privileging Western European paradigms and repertoire despite teachers' claims that they did not espouse such beliefs. Rohan concluded:

> Teachers may think one thing, but the organizational structures they work within, pedagogical decisions they make, and the language they use to talk about music, give conflicting and confusing messages. In particular, the realities of assessment requirements, the demands of

competitions, the limiting structure of performance-based programs are all examples of "actions" that speak very loudly, drowning out more inclusive messages.

(p. 299)

In the North Side Choir, an additive approach to multicultural music education, which privileges Western classical music by placing it as the core of the curriculum, contributed to students' perceptions of the superiority of Western classical music. The emphasis placed on Western classical repertoire, notational fluency, and the Western European style of singing were "actions" that spoke loudly, at times "drowning out" their teacher's messages that cultural diversity was valued within the North Side Choir.

References

Banks, J. A. (2005). Approaches to multicultural curriculum reform. In J. A. Banks & C. A. M. Banks (Eds.), *Multicultural education: Issues and perspectives* (5th ed., pp. 242–261). Hoboken, NJ: Wiley.

Dweck, C. S. (2006). *Mindset: The new psychology of success.* New York, NY: Random House.

Gay, G. (2002). Preparing for culturally responsive teaching. *Journal of Teacher Education, 53*(2), 106–116.

Karlsen, S. (2013). Immigrant students and the "homeland music": Meanings, negotiations, and implications. *Research Studies in Music Education, 35*(2), 161–177. https://doi.org/10.1177/1321103X13508057

Lopez, G. (2001). The value of hard work: Lessons on parent involvement from an (im)migrant household. *Harvard Educational Review, 71*(3), 416–437.

Rohan, T. J. (2011). *Teaching music, learning culture: The challenge of culturally responsive music education* (Doctoral dissertation). Retrieved from http://hdl.handle.net/10523/1865

Root, M. P. (2004). Multiracial families and children: Implications for educational research and practice. In J. A. Banks & C. A. M. Banks (Eds.), *Handbook of research on multicultural education* (2nd ed.). San Francisco, CA: Jossey-Bass.

Shaw, J. T. (2015). "Knowing their world": Urban choral music educators' knowledge of context. *Journal of Research in Music Education, 63*(2), 198–223. https://doi.org/10.1177/0022429415584377

Suárez-Orozco, C., & Suárez-Orozco, M. M. (2001). *Children of immigration* (1st ed.). Cambridge, MA: Harvard University Press.

Suárez-Orozco, C., Suárez-Orozco, M. M., & Doucet, F. (2004). The academic engagement and achievement of Latino youth. In J. A. Banks & C. A. M. Banks (Eds.), *Handbook of research on multicultural education* (2nd ed., pp. 420–440). San Francisco, CA: Jossey-Bass.

Thibeault, M. D. (2009). The violin and the fiddle: Narratives of music and musician in a high-school setting. In C. R. Abril & J. L. Kerchner (Eds.), *Musical experience in our lives: Things we learn and meanings we make* (pp. 255–276). Lanham, MD: Rowman & Littlefield.

Valdés, G. (1996). *Con respeto: Bridging the distances between culturally diverse families and schools.* New York, NY: Teachers College Press.

4 Culturally Responsive Teaching in the South Side Choir

The South Side Choir was situated in a predominantly African American community. As I drove to rehearsals each Monday, vacant, boarded-up properties were marked with red Xs indicating that the buildings had been condemned. Forty-seven of the large metropolitan district's schools, located in predominately African American communities, had closed within the past two years after being designated "underperforming" according to policy emphasizing standardized test scores. Bright yellow signs dotted the landscape, designating adult-monitored "safe passage zones," through which students could walk to school. Families of students displaced by school closures still worried that children would have to travel though areas with high gang- or drug-related activity in order to attend school.

Teacher-conductor Lionel Mitchell's descriptions of the community focused on its positive attributes: organizations that provided valuable services, community leaders who inspired the neighborhood's youth, public school teachers and administrators who were "exceptional," and students who were "ready to sing" and "excited to learn." While emphasizing these assets, he noted that school and community safety concerns remained salient:

> This neighborhood is a crime-infested area of the city, very poverty-stricken. People would even label it the disenfranchised part of the city. I'm just gonna be real with you, it is very dangerous for these kids after a certain hour. Some people are even so bold to commit heinous crimes in daylight. . . . It's scary, even, to think about the kids walking from school just to get home, and home may be just a block or two away. It's a harsh reality, but the schools have some exceptional teachers and administrators who are really trying to give these kids a better future.

Demographic information for the choir is presented in Table 1.2. All of the students self-identified as African American except for one, Gianna, who identified as Latina. Recognizing that a majority of the community's residents met the federal designation of "living in poverty," the organization did not request information about students' socioeconomic status.

Teacher's Biographical Sketch: "If Mr. Mitchell Is Well Rounded, We Can Be Too"

Mr. Mitchell shared his African American background with the majority of his students. He considered his formative musical experiences to be "rooted in the church," having grown up singing gospel there. He held a Bachelor of Arts with emphases in vocal performance, voice pedagogy, and choral conducting and a Master of Music in vocal performance. Upon completing his master's, he taught K–12 music in a private school located in a southern state for three years. He then decided to return to the city in which he had grown up because he felt a sense of personal responsibility to serve that community.

Mr. Mitchell's multifaceted cultural and musical identity enabled him to both relate to his students and broaden their horizons:

> I'm very proud of spirituals, gospel music, my church background, and where I come from. I don't let it fall second to art song, classical, opera, sacred choral anthems. . . . All of those things are a part of me and I want them [students] to experience all those styles of music. . . . I think they're gonna see that if Mr. Mitchell is well rounded, we can be too. He can go from jamming, dancing, and playing hip-hop songs with us, then all of a sudden, he can play "Art Thou Troubled?" by Handel and he's showing us how to do ornamentation. I want them to walk away remembering that I stood out because I was able to do many styles of music skillfully.

Elements of Mr. Mitchell's Culturally Responsive Practice

Knowledge of Cultural Diversity and Culturally Responsive Caring

Mr. Mitchell's experiences growing up in an African American community located geographically close to the one in which he taught contributed personal practical knowledge relevant to his teaching. He viewed his role as a "life coach," frequently engaging students in "real-life talks":

> I'm very open with my kids, because I want them to know that Mr. Mitchell didn't have a perfect life, didn't grow up in the best neighborhood, didn't always have food to eat. . . . I've shared with them experiences where I was held at gunpoint. We've had to have realistic, real-life talks like that. I want them to know that they have an advocate in me, an adult who can say, "I know what you're going through, you're not alone, this is how you can handle that situation."

(Shaw, 2018, p. 191)

His pedagogy reflected a deep, personal understanding of his African American students' learning needs arising from parallels in their cultural backgrounds. He related:

> We have some connections where I know how they feel and why they have questions. Why they have hang-ups about authority with teachers and police officers. . . . In my line of work, as an African American male with a master's degree teaching these kids, I get pulled over by the police at least 4 or 5 times a year. . . . It really does hurt. Sometimes it feels like it doesn't matter how much I achieve, I will always have this stereotype pinned on my back.
>
> Unfortunately, in our African American community, we have to develop a code of behavior for when these situations happen, even if it's unjust. I have to prepare them in a very no-nonsense way. That makes me more firm because I know they have a lot of obstacles stacked against them before they get a chance to grow up. We have a deeper connection that way. . . . The connection that I make sets up a space where a life might be saved [because students will be] more informed when these situations come up.
>
> (Shaw, 2018, p. 191)

Beyond focusing on musical content and concerns during class, Mr. Mitchell frequently coached students on how to handle situations such as being accused of cheating on a test, being stopped by police, and responding to racist comments. Through "real life talks" such as these, Mr. Mitchell explicitly taught students to navigate a "culture of power" without compromising their cultural identity, a characteristic of teachers who work effectively with pupils of color (Delpit, 1995; Ladson-Billings, 1994).

Designing Culturally Relevant Curricula

Mr. Mitchell developed students' cultural competence by integrating music that honored the cultural heritages of specific students into his curriculum, noting, "Especially in a choir where multiple races and ethnicities are represented, how could I not pick a piece that is unique to that person's heritage?" Observing that "in some situations, kids don't even know that certain songs are unique to their heritage," he considered opportunities for students to grow in understanding and appreciation for their own cultural backgrounds to be vitally important. In addition, he sought to expand students' cultural and musical horizons: "My goal is that they get a well-rounded repertoire and education. Be it jazz, gospel, music from a Jewish tradition, from Latin culture, from South Africa. . . . I want them to experience all of those."

Mr. Mitchell emphasized that developing culturally relevant curricula requires more than promoting a mere surface acquaintance with repertoire representing diverse cultural traditions:

> More than just singing folklore unique to that group, multicultural education is when you study, understand, appreciate and respect another person's background and culture. . . . I can get up and sing *"Bakesh Shalom"* all day, but still have an attitude about Jewish culture. . . . There definitely has to be a social dynamic that goes along with studying and singing the music.

Fostering students' deep understanding of the social, cultural, historical, and political context surrounding repertoire and using choral literature as a vehicle for social emotional learning were aspects of the "social dynamic" Mr. Mitchell advocated. He explained, "I want them to walk away with an understanding of the historical context and make social, emotional connections to the music."

Cultural Congruity in Instruction

The following field note excerpt offers a glimpse of Mr. Mitchell's rehearsals, illustrating strategies he used to promote cultural congruity, particularly relating to notational fluency and vocal timbre.

> Mr. Mitchell gestured for students to step-touch as he played the piano introduction for "Revelation 19," a gospel piece several singers obviously knew well. He modeled each phrase in a soulful style, inviting students to imitate him. As students learned the song aurally, the teacher's verbal instructions were minimal and students were continuously engaged in singing.
>
> Next, Mr. Mitchell asked students to look at their music for "May Joyful Music Fill the Air," an arrangement based on a canon by Tallis, which featured two vocal parts notated on separate staves. When a student volunteer read the text aloud, she read each line twice so that some phrases repeated. Mr. Mitchell responded: "She's not wrong, but we have a certain way of reading two parts," going on to explain the concept of systems in a choral octavo. He demonstrated how to sing the melody, demonstrating *bel canto* technique, and challenging students to notice when he breathed. They listened attentively, marking breaths in their scores. Mr. Mitchell explained that most of the note values students had been hearing lasted for one beat. He challenged them to listen again and identify the longest note in the song. The students located the longest note, and Mr. Mitchell directed them to write the number two above it to indicate its length. He explained that this was called a half note while notes lasting for one beat are quarter notes.
>
> "Sing with me," Mr. Mitchell invited. The students sang lower than expected, attempting to match the octave in which he had modeled. He

responded, "Okay. In your range," demonstrating the desired octave. Singers reacted by laughing uncomfortably. Mr. Mitchell, exhibiting a playful attitude, responded, "Yes, I can sing in your range!" The singers laughed again, seeming more comfortable. Borrowing a phrase from rapper and hip-hop artist Jay-Z, Mr. Mitchell asked students, "Can I get a woop woop?" They answered, "Woop woop!" engaging their chest voices. He responded, "Good! Now try it this way." Using head voice, he modeled, "Can I get a woop woop?" The students responded "Woop woop" in head voice with a lighter quality more suggestive of classical singing. "There' s a method to this madness," Mr. Mitchell explained as he alternated between having the singers say "woop woop" using "Jay-Z style" versus "classical style." He invited students to sing the whole melody, explaining that singing this particular melody should feel the same as saying "woop woop" in classical style. As they finished, singers spontaneously applauded and appeared pleased with their progress.

An emphasis on notational fluency is a curricular norm with potential to be discontinuous with students' experiences outside of music education settings (Bradley, 2006; Carlow, 2004; Joyce, 2003; Kelly-McHale, 2011; Rohan, 2011; Thibeault, 2009). Noting that many of his students had extensive experience singing gospel in church choirs where they typically learned music aurally, Mr. Mitchell taught music theory and sight-singing without permitting these norms to dominate the curriculum. For example, he taught "May Joyful Music Fill the Air" through a partially oral process, providing students opportunities to develop notational fluency while continuing to use the aural learning strategies with which many were experienced. He balanced score-centered experiences, such as with "May Joyful Music Fill the Air," with ones in which students learned aurally, as with "Revelation 19." Further, he opened rehearsal with an experience likely to be in students' wheelhouses: A gospel selection with which many students were familiar, taught through an oral process that for many was a preferred learning strategy, and featuring a style of singing that aligned with many singers' preferred vocal models.

Previous research has suggested that students may perceive the Western classical style of singing typically emphasized in North American choral music organizations as being incongruent with their singing experiences outside of choir (Bradley, 2006; Chinn, 1997; Joyce, 2003). This point was particularly salient within Mr. Mitchell's choir, as he explained:

> Because we're working with predominately Black children, their influences do come from hip-hop music, from church music, and from the way their parents sing and speak. . . . They don't really have experience singing in head voice where you find a lot of traditional choral music, especially for treble voices. Those nice floaty phrases, high notes, and even florid singing—it's just not found in the Black church.

They're intimidated by it at first because it's unusual for them. We have to tell them, "Okay, this is what's happening. Your voice wants to switch registers". . . . [I] explain it to them in a way that they understand, "I'm gonna have to flip over into head voice because I'm not comfortable singing that high D above middle C [in chest voice]." It's mental building blocks like that.

Students' discussion of this topic permeated classroom and interview conversations. They first broached the subject while discussing *"Shalom Chaverim"*:

Student 1:	If I go too high it makes my head hurt because I'm trying to force myself to do something.
Student 2:	You can't force yourself to do something that you cannot do.
Student 1:	Right.
Student 3:	Like, it's good to go along with the song and beat and make your voice go higher and lower, but too high is not good.
Julia:	Is *"Shalom"* one of the highest songs you have?
Student 2:	Yes. That's one of the really challenging songs.
Student 1:	The different pitches are really hard to hit. Like with *"Shalom"* we have to stretch our *"O's"* a little more like when we're fancy and maybe our style is our style.
Julia:	So your teacher's asking you to use a different style of singing? He wants you to form the vowels a certain way?
Student 1:	Right.
Student 3:	And a lot of people can't do that.
Student 2:	Right. We wanna make our voices connect all together by using our regular voice and our regular notes.

Thus, three features of classically oriented vocal technique presented barriers to these students: a range they perceived to be high, head voice, and tall, round vowels. Aware of his students' perceptions, Mr. Mitchell selected a substantial amount of repertoire that showcased students' "regular voices," including pieces such as Jeffrey LaValley's "Revelation 19," Curtis Mayfield's "People Get Ready," and Israel Houghton's "Not Forgotten." The African American students I interviewed perceived these selections, all of which were composed by African American artists and representative of African American musical traditions, to be relevant to their cultural identities.

Although Mr. Mitchell provided opportunities for students to showcase preferred performance styles through music they considered culturally relevant, he also challenged them to learn repertoire, vocal timbres, and musical skills that they had not previously explored. The previous field note excerpt illustrates one technique he used to facilitate a style shift from the vocal timbre and style appropriate for "Revelation 19," with which students were familiar and comfortable, toward the Western classical style of singing emphasized in "May Joyful Music Fill the Air." Referencing a vocal model his students considered culturally relevant, he had singers experience the less-familiar vocal register in "Jay-Z style" before attempting it with "classical style." He had them practice switching between the two styles, using humor and a playful approach to diffuse tension or insecurity associated with exploring a less-familiar vocal technique. This strategy offers an example of "cultural scaffolding" in a choral context (Gay, 2002, p. 109).

Sociopolitical Consciousness

Mr. Mitchell's practice also exemplified Ladson-Billings' (2002) notion of developing sociopolitical consciousness. He primarily approached this aim via structured classroom dialogue through which students recognized and challenged stereotypic thinking, engaged in social critique, and discussed actions they could take toward solving issues of importance to them. In addition to selecting choral literature according to students' musical and developmental needs, he considered its potential to spark discussion about social issues:

> A lot of music we did this year was protest songs, especially because there were a lot of situations going on with deaths in Ferguson, Staten Island, Baltimore, Chicago, St. Louis . . . at the hands of police officers. . . . These kids, they're very impressionable at this age, and they're seeing these things, and they're asking all of these questions. . . . The music really lends itself to opening up about current issues . . . we always talk about the Trayvon Martins.[1] There's situations where the music, like "Ain't Gonna Let Nobody Turn Me 'Round," "Woke Up This Morning With My Mind Stayed On Freedom," "People Get Ready." . . . This kind of music really allows me to engage the kids socially and emotionally, and ask them, "What are some situations in your life where we need change right now?" When you allow that kind of conversation to happen, they open up and start sharing things about themselves and their families. Without that kind of engagement, I don't think the kids truly grasp the full concept of what they're singing or studying. You have to make it relevant.
> (Shaw, 2018, p. 195)

Understanding the relevance of the Black Lives Matter movement to his students' lived experiences, Mr. Mitchell planned learning experiences that opened avenues for students' reflection on, self-expression about, and discussion of that movement. These experiences provided opportunities for students to engage with sociopolitical issues with guidance from a caring adult figure. Following are portraits of three singers whose experiences offer insight into CRT as practiced in the South Side Choir.

Zoey: "Singing Is About Expressing Feelings"

Zoey, a precocious and gregarious fifth grader, was one of the first singers to join the South Side Choir. She described herself as "smart" and "inspirational," emphasizing that she's "got swagger." Her family included three generations of female singers. Zoey sang in her church's adult choir and had been a proud member of her school's choir until the program was discontinued due to insufficient funding. She previously studied violin through a community music organization. While she no longer took private lessons, she continued to play the violin, piano, and guitar for enjoyment.

Outside of choir, Zoey learned music by listening to songs repeatedly and "playing around" until she could recreate them with her voice or at the keyboard. She had limited patience for learning to read notation because it didn't feel efficient. She claimed, "The notes are really hard and it's just kind of too much. When you have a song and you're learning it, you want to learn it today." She enjoyed composing her own songs and devised her own notation:

> I like to write songs. They just pop up in my head. . . . Some I write down and some I don't. I'll write numbers on the [piano] keys because I don't really do reading music, so I just go off the numbers. I write what goes on in the world. . . . It's fun.

Zoey used music as an avenue for self-expression, emphasizing that singing is really "about expressing feelings." Her rich musical life inside and outside of choir led to her positive self-identification as a musician and singer.

In interviews, Zoey described the importance of her cultural background to her sense of self:

Zoey: I am Native American Choctaw Indian, African American, and beautiful.
Julia: And beautiful, of course. [Zoey laughs]. Do you think it's important to identify yourself as Choctaw Indian or African-American?
Zoey: Yes, because people need to know about me. I don't want to be the person that is interviewed, but it's not really me. I like to be myself and if people don't like me, then they're missing out on a whole lot.

She considered her cultural identity to be an essential aspect of her "real" self and wanted to ensure that our interviews accurately reflected who she is by acknowledging her cultural identity.

Zoey's preferred musical genres included hip-hop, pop, and R&B. She identified Alicia Keys as the singer she most desired to emulate. She considered Keys to be "inspiring" because:

> She sings in her own style . . . she plays a little bit. Sometimes she writes a song and at first, it sounds like this [sings to demonstrate]. Then maybe when she performs [later], she has a different version. She has the right tune, but she kind of goes up and down and side-to-side.

Zoey proceeded to demonstrate this concept, singing three melodic variations of a phrase from "Girl on Fire" by sliding between and bending pitches, adding stylistic elements associated with African American singing. When asked if she had opportunities to practice singing like Alicia Keys in choir, Zoey replied: "No, not at all. We don't get to sing freely. We stick to what the song is like." She would have appreciated freedom to experiment with stylistic elements such as those she demonstrated, "but not too much so that it doesn't even sound like the song." She further expressed frustration that the necessity of blending within a choral context limited her freedom of expression. To Zoey, stylistic freedom was an important aspect of "singing with her regular voice."

As she listened to the recording of Purcell's "Sound the Trumpet," she reacted especially to the vocal range, style, and timbre demonstrated in the recording:

Julia: How would you react if your teacher wanted you to sound like that?
Zoey: Well . . . [shaking her head]. I'm gonna stick with my own voice . . . 'cause I don't like some of the songs we sing 'cause we sing too high. It's not high for me; I just don't like to sing high like that.
Julia: Mm hmm. So you could sing high like that . . .
Zoey: Yes. I could if I wanted to.
Julia: But you don't want to?
Zoey: But I don't want to.
Julia: Would those singers fit in with this choir?
Zoey: No. That's not what they're usually singing [in the South Side Choir] . . . They're good singers, but they wouldn't fit in because of their pitch.
Julia: Can you describe what you think those singers might look like?
Zoey: Um, the opposite race of me.
Julia: They're White?
Zoey: Yes. I don't like to say that word.
Julia: Okay. What would you say instead?
Zoey: Non-colored. Opposite race.

Discussing the Purcell recording prompted Zoey to share her impressions of a recent related experience:

Zoey: On Thursday I saw "The Nutcracker" 'cause my school went. That [recording] reminds me of when the fairy princesses [danced]. They sang during that part. There was only one girl that was Black.
Julia: How did that feel, to see that? You've been a ballet dancer, right?
Zoey: Yeah . . . I think a lot of Black people are not interested really in ballet.
Julia: Why would there be only one African American ballet dancer?
Zoey: Maybe she was interested 'cause I was a ballet dancer. I was the only Black person in my class.
Julia: How did that feel?
Zoey: I felt left out. I didn't really have any friends at ballet.

Zoey's assumption that the recording of "Sound the Trumpet," which exemplified the Western classical style of singing, featured White singers is noteworthy. She associated the style of singing featured in the Purcell recording with that used in Tchaikovsky's Nutcracker Suite during the "Waltz of the Snowflakes," which similarly features treble voices, *bel canto* vocal technique, and extensive use of head voice. For Zoey, this mental association included an image of the dancers she saw on stage during the singing, only one of whom was African American. She associated the more classically oriented style of singing with two art forms in which African Americans are underrepresented: classical music and ballet. Her impressions were informed by her personal experience as a ballet dancer, during which she was the only African American in her class and felt she "didn't really have any friends." She seemed not only to associate Western classical singing with a White way of singing, but with feelings of exclusion.

Zoey's musical preferences and vocal models were consistent with prior researchers' findings that African American students often prefer African American genres (McCrary, 1993, 2000; McCrary & Gauthier, 1995; Morrison, 1998; Walker, 2006; Ward-Steinman, 2006) and vocal models (Chinn, 1997; Killian, 1990). In her preferred vocal model, Zoey admired stylistic qualities such as glides, bends, dips, and exploitation of chest register, which are associated with African American singing (Burnim & Maultsby, 1987; Chinn, 1997). This pattern of findings supports additional authors' assertions that cultural values and traditions comprise one possible influence on students' vocal self-identification (Chinn, 1997; Haskell, 1987; Joyce, 2003).

Of further interest is the fact that Zoey equated the Western classical style of singing with a White way of singing, which she associated with feelings of marginalization and exclusion. Although she believed she could sing like the Purcell recording, she had no desire to do so, preferring to "stick with her own voice." As these impressions were shared by more than one participant, relationships between vocal timbre and cultural identity are explored further in this and the next chapter.

One choral experience Zoey identified as being responsive to her cultural identity was her study of the South African anti-apartheid song, *"Thula Sizwe."* Mr. Mitchell explained his reasons for selecting this piece for the choir to study and perform:

> This song is actually a peaceful protest song. . . . I was telling [students] how there are a lot of parallels between the apartheid system and what we went through with Jim Crow and civil rights. They could make the connections and see where the inequities lie, and how music was utilized to stand against these kinds of regimes. They start to really find those kinds of connections and then it becomes more personal. The message is more enduring for them.

Zoey considered the process of learning and performing *"Thula Sizwe"* to be relevant to her Choctaw Indian heritage. To elucidate the connection between the song and that facet of her cultural identity, she described a performance she had attended where one performer sang about his experiences of oppression in relation to his Native American heritage:

> At the performance, there was this young man. He was Native American. [He sang:] "They was [sic] all the people that were taking our land." I could connect to him. . . . That one reminded me of what my great aunt went through because she grew up like he did. . . . I think we should learn about what he's talking about.

Thus, Zoey perceived the South African anti-apartheid song, *"Thula Sizwe"* to relate to her Choctaw Indian heritage in that both cultural groups had experienced a history of colonization and oppression, which she believed was important to learn about and explicitly recognize in the curriculum. She considered such opportunities "important" because:

> You hear about your culture; you know more about what your culture's about . . . we should learn about the music, because that's what some of our family went through. . . . It tells me what life was like and it explains the present, too.

Jazmin: "My Music Is About Me, To Make Me Feel Better"

Jazmin, a ten-year-old fifth grader, described herself as "kind" and "loving." She definitely self-identified as African American. She had a rich musical life outside of choir, much of which revolved around singing. Her family affirmed her identity as a singer, recognizing her ability and requesting performances at family gatherings. Jazmin noted that she "sang everywhere" including school choir, church choir, at home, and in the shower.

She observed that her choir directors at school and church had "mixed it up" by having the choirs sing stylistically diverse repertoire, but noted that her experiences singing at church especially emphasized gospel and R&B. She also danced for her church's praise team, relating, "I dance fluently." Noticing that the word "graceful" permeated Jazmin's descriptions of herself, her singing, and her dancing, I asked her to explain what that word meant to her. She replied, "Graceful means when you just let your emotions out and thank God [for the] things that you been through and God changed them." By singing and dancing "gracefully," Jazmin expressed her spirituality.

We discussed how Jazmin's singing experiences differed inside and outside of choir:

Julia: What kinds of music do you sing when you're not at choir?
Jazmin: I sing our music, you know how they be rapping on the radio and stuff.
Julia: You don't get to do that here necessarily?

Jazmin: No, not at all.
Julia: Is there anything else that you like to sing that you never do here in choir?
Jazmin: My own songs that I make up. Sometimes I get angry. I start crying and then I'll make up songs.
Julia: To let your emotions out?
Jazmin: Yeah. I write it down with pen. I just mix up the words and make them into a song. I use my piano. I use my mom's phone sometimes [to record them].

Jazmin used the label "our music" to describe her preferred musical genres, which included rap, hip-hop, and R&B. She supposed that the reason they didn't typically sing "her music" in choir was because of inappropriate lyrics and subject matter. She explained, "My music is way out of proportion. It's got curse words. It's rap music." Summarizing the purpose music served in her life, she remarked, "my music is more about me, to make me feel better."

Jazmin's definition of "singer" centered upon vocal range and register:

Julia: What makes somebody a singer?
Jazmin: How they sing high and low in a different tone of voice.
Julia: Can you give me an example of what using different tones of voice would be?
Jazmin: Chest voice, head voice, high voice, low voice.
Julia: Do you consider yourself to be a singer?
Jazmin: [Affirmatively] Mmm-hmm.
Julia: Because you can do those things?
Jazmin: [Nods head.]

Beyoncé was a singer Jazmin especially wanted to emulate because she admired her extensive range and ability to sing effectively in both chest voice and head voice.

Her reactions to the recording of "Sound the Trumpet" also centered upon vocal range and register:

Julia: What if Mr. Mitchell brought that in, played it for the class, and said, "We're going to learn how to sing like this"?
Jazmin: I would be way confused.
Julia: What would be confusing to you?
Jazmin: That when they're high, they stay at the high voice for a while, and I wouldn't be able to do that.
Julia: Okay, so did you say "high" voice or "head" voice?
Jazmin: Both.
Julia: Do you think you could learn how to do that?
Jazmin: Not really.

Julia: No? Would you want to?
Jazmin: Yeah.
Julia: Okay. What do you think those kids might look like?
Jazmin: Caucasian.

Zoey and Jazmin, both of whom identified as African American, were the only student participants to discuss the imagined appearance of singers featured in the vocal model recordings in terms of race or ethnicity. Both associated the Western classical style of singing demonstrated in the Purcell recording with Caucasian singers. Specifically, the vocal attributes Jazmin equated with a White style of singing included a high vocal range and extensive use of head voice. Although she may have lacked self-efficacy concerning her ability to sing high and in head voice, she expressed interest in learning to sing in the style featured in the recording. Interestingly, she considered herself a singer because she could sing with "different tones of voice," meaning "chest voice, head voice, high voice, low voice." She exhibited willingness to cross style parameters, and an ability to style shift was beginning to shape her self-definition as a singer.

When invited to describe learning experiences she considered culturally responsive, Jazmin identified *"Thula Sizwe"* as a piece she considered relevant to her identity as an African American. She related the piece to the United States' history of racial segregation:

Julia: Is there any music that lets you express being African American?
Jazmin: *"Thula Sizwe."*
Julia: Can you tell me in your own words what the words in *"Thula Sizwe"* mean?
Jazmin: *"Thula Sizwe"* means "Hush, nation. Don't cry. Your Jehovah will conquer for you freedom."
Julia: So what does that mean to you?
Jazmin: That back in the day, people couldn't express they selves by talking. They expressed they self by singing together and marching, so it really sends out a note to some, that "Don't cry, Jesus will conquer for you. He will make things better."
Julia: So that connects to being African American for you?
Jazmin: Yeah.
Julia: In what way?
Jazmin: That it was slavery for us and the Whites got to control us. . . . So, I just felt like that song is sending notes out to how they was treated back in the day.

Root (2004) asserted that "regional and generational history of race and ethnic relations" comprises a macro lens through which additional experiences of identity are screened (p. 116), an observation relevant to Zoey's and Jazmin's experiences in that they self-identified with two groups that have historically been oppressed and marginalized in U.S. society: Choc-taw Indians and African Americans. Both girls perceived music that recog-nized and challenged oppression as being culturally relevant, even when the music did not correspond precisely to their African American or Choctaw Indian ancestry. Their perspectives suggest that learning experiences inviting artistic expression about racism, inequity, and oppression may be culturally or politically relevant to students who have experienced marginalization or oppression.

Gianna: "You Don't Know if You Want To Be Latina or American"

Eleven-year-old fifth grader Gianna described herself as "creative," "gener-ous," and "active," explaining:

> My creative part comes from my artistic side because my dad knows how to draw. So that inspires me to become an artist, but I also wanna sing. The generous part is that if anyone feels hurt, I ask them how they feel.

In addition to choir, she participated in gymnastics, swimming, and guitar lessons. Gianna considered herself a musician because she "understood what she was singing" and "felt what songs were telling her." She used music as an avenue for self-expression, telling the audience "her story."

As the only Latina, she stood out in a choir that reflected the demo-graphic composition of the predominately African American surround-ing community. She described her experiences as the only Latina choir member:

Gianna: At first I felt really scared, because I didn't know how they [peers] were gonna treat me. Then, as I started to know them, I felt really good. Now, I really feel safe with this group.

Julia: What do you think teachers need to know about what it is like to have a different cultural background than the majority of the class?

Gianna: If I were the teacher, I would make him or her feel very comfort-able and feel that they're gonna be safe here.

She explained that icebreakers, team-building activities, and class discussions Mr. Mitchell facilitated during rehearsals contributed toward creating a classroom environment that felt "safe."

When asked to name a singer that she most wanted to emulate, Gianna chose Selena Gomez because she perceived her to be stylistically versatile. She noted "she doesn't just go for one type of music." When I asked Gianna how she would react if Mr. Mitchell asked the choir to sing in that style featured in the "Sound the Trumpet" recording, she responded:

> I would react very normal because we sing like that in choir. . . . Mr. Mitchell teaches us how to make our voice into head voice, so yes, I really like singing head voice because you kind of sound like an opera.

When we discussed Mr. Mitchell's preferred vocal model, Gianna explained that attempting to sing like that recording would be "difficult because they sing in chest voice a lot . . . but it would be a cool thing to try out." As the following exchange demonstrates, she believed that emulating her teacher's recording would require her to attempt a challenging style shift:

Julia: Do you think that you could be taught to sing like that?
Gianna: No.
Julia: How come?
Gianna: I've tried to sing in a chest voice, but it really doesn't come out very well. When I try it usually starts as chest voice, but then it goes into head voice, so . . .
Julia: Would you like to be able to sing like that with your chest voice?
Gianna: I would like it because it would be a cool, new thing that you would have in your voice. My family would be very proud because they would know that I have two different kinds of voices.

Gianna was convinced that any of the singers to whom we listened would fit in as members of the South Side Choir. She observed, "We have different types of voices, so they would fit in. . . . The teacher would help. He would know or find a place where they would fit in."

Gianna was a second-generation immigrant, having been born in the United States to Honduran parents. The following exchange illuminates aspects of her cultural identity:

Gianna: I was born in the United States, but my parents were born in Honduras. So, it's fun learning new things from where my mom and dad were from. I've always wanted to visit there.
Julia: Your parents teach you about Honduras?
Gianna: Yeah, and my grandparents. My grandfather tells us stories about what has happened there over the years and new stuff they're doing. Like right now they're voting and getting a new president, so it's interesting.
Julia: How would you describe your own cultural identity?
Gianna: Well, I think Latina because it's fun learning new vocabulary in Spanish. At home, my mom speaks Spanish and a little bit of English. It's fun that she's learning my language and I'm learning her language.

Julia: Do you think it's important to identify yourself as a Latina?
Gianna: You want to be both of them, like you don't know if you want to be Latina or American because it's so fun learning both of their languages that you don't know which one to pick.
Julia: Do you feel like it's possible to be both, or do you feel like you'd have to make a choice?
Gianna: I think it's possible that you can be both.
Julia: Mm hmm, but you feel torn between the two?
Gianna: Yeah.

Gianna described feeling conflicted between identifying with American and Honduran culture, an experience shared by many second-generation immigrants (Olneck, 2004; Suárez-Orozco, Suárez-Orozco, & Todorova, 2008). She enjoyed learning about her Honduran background from her parents and grandparents and discussing Honduran politics with her grandfather. However, she also felt connected to American culture, having been born, experienced childhood, and attended public schools in the United States. She believed "it's possible that you can be both," suggesting that she was crafting a "hyphenated identity" in which she balanced her Honduran identity on one side with her American identity on the other (Suárez-Orozco, Suárez-Orozco, & Doucet, 2004).

Gianna used the pan-ethnic descriptor "Latina" to describe her cultural identity. Our discussion of whether music related to her cultural identity revealed that language was a significant experiential piece of cultural identity for Gianna:

Julia: You said, "Sometimes I feel more American. Sometimes I feel more Honduran like my parents." Does music ever help you feel American or Honduran?
Gianna: No.
Julia: So, music doesn't necessarily connect to your cultural identity?
Gianna: No, it's kind of . . . the place I'm in. Because in school we usually just talk English and I'm learning new things about English, so it makes me feel more English than Honduran. When I get home, we start just talking Spanish and I get to understand more of what I came from.

Gianna experienced and expressed cultural identity situationally, depending on "the place she was in." In school, surrounded by English-speaking peers, she "felt more English." Having never lived in or visited Honduras herself, speaking Spanish at home was a primary way she maintained a connection with her parental culture of origin.

Gianna's grandmother encouraged musical connections with her Honduran heritage:

Gianna: My grandma knows I'm in the choir because she got very excited that I had gotten in. So now she's teaching me new songs because over here [in choir], we're learning German songs. So probably one day we'll be singing a Spanish song. Then I'll probably be knowing that song, so my grandma's gonna keep teaching me that.

Julia: Have you done a song in Spanish yet?

Gianna: No, not yet.

Although Gianna did not perceive her experiences in choir to be responsive to her own cultural identity, she appreciated opportunities Mr. Mitchell provided to learn about cultures beyond the realm of her prior experiences. She especially enjoyed learning *"Thula Sizwe,"* remarking:

> It was from a different place that I didn't know about, so I felt very good that I was learning a different thing. I feel good because I have my parents from Honduras, but I'm still learning Zulu. So you combine them together and you get something huge.

Unlike her African American peers, Gianna did not associate the Western classical style of singing with a White way of singing. She was open to learning about and style shifting between multiple styles of singing, as evidenced by her comments that "it would be a cool thing" and "her family would be proud" if she could learn to sing with "different kinds of voices." She viewed crossing style parameters as an additive process through which she gained "something huge."

Pedagogical actions that were culturally relevant to the African American classroom majority did not result in CRT for Gianna, the only Latina in the South Side Choir. While musical experiences that might have fostered Gianna's cultural competence had not yet been explored in the choir, she appreciated the psychologically safe learning environment her teacher had established as well as opportunities to learn about cultures different from her own. She expressed interest in connecting to her Honduran heritage musically, and her grandmother was beginning to foster such connections outside of choir. Considering that she maintained a connection to Honduran culture through the Spanish language, opportunities to sing in Spanish during choir might have been meaningful to her.

While responding to the classroom majority may present a logical point of departure for CRT, teachers should remain alert to the potential risk of alienating students who do not identify with the classroom majority. Prior research has also cautioned that students' ethnic majority/minority status in the classroom can affect the frequency and intensity of their participation in class activities and interactions with peers (McCrary, 2000). Students who hold ethnic minority status within their classroom therefore deserve teachers' thoughtful consideration and proactive planning. Teachers can ensure that students belonging to classroom minority groups receive equitable opportunities to engage with music they find culturally relevant. They can guide classroom discussions with purposeful attention toward ensuring that students who belong to classroom minority groups receive equitable opportunities to contribute. They can guard against placing students who belong to classroom minority groups in compromising social situations with their peers (Karlsen, 2013). They can also attend to the quality of social interaction within choral ensembles, paying particular attention to whether classroom minority students find the environment to be genuinely welcoming and inclusive. Social events, icebreakers, and teambuilding activities that build singers' relationships, trust, and rapport merit the same degree of strategic planning as does the process of planning a season's musical events.

CRT in the South Side Choir: Overarching Themes

"We Want To Sing With Our Regular Voices":
Vocal Timbre and Cultural Identity

Singers in the South Side Choir preferred vocal models that shared their race, ethnicity, and gender, findings consistent with prior researchers' observations (Chinn, 1997; Killian, 1990). Jazmin's and Zoey's preferences for African American genres, performers, and vocal models supported Chinn's (1997) assertion that "African American adolescent females may identify with vocal characteristics demonstrated by singers whose style is representative of African American musical heritage" (p. 637). Mr. Mitchell's African American students had plentiful opportunities to sing music representative of their cultural backgrounds. These occasions built on their cultural knowledge and showcased their preferred performance styles, thus promoting cultural competence.

Chinn (1997) cautioned that African American "young women, whose vocal identities may be related to their ethnicity and values, may not trust a choral educator who attempts to teach them to sing in other vocal styles" (p. 637). To the contrary, Mr. Mitchell was able to encourage his African American students to cross style parameters and perform repertoire that was less culturally familiar to them. For example, within one concert, his students performed "People Get Ready," *"Thula Sizwe,"* "Not Forgotten," and "Revelation 19," all of which highlighted performance styles his African American students preferred. However, in the same program, students performed Praetorius' *"Jubilate Deo,"* Randall Thompson's "Velvet Shoes," and an arrangement of a canon by Thomas Tallis with a Western classical style of singing, experiences of which they were equally proud. Their experiences suggest that opportunities to demonstrate culturally preferred performance styles may enhance students' receptivity toward additional styles, including but not limited to the Western classical tradition.

Several aspects of Mr. Mitchell's CRT may have encouraged his students' openness toward crossing culturally informed style parameters. First, through experiences that developed cultural competence, he affirmed students' preferred styles of singing as valid expressions of their cultural identities.

Among a range of musical role models he presented as part of the symbolic curriculum, he emphasized vocal models students considered culturally relevant. These included vocal models of the same race, ethnicity, and/or gender as the students as well as individuals students identified as preferred vocal models. He also frequently used a process of cultural scaffolding when introducing vocal timbres and styles with which students had less experience. That is, he used familiar musical and cultural elements as pedagogical bridges toward learning music beyond the realm of students' prior experiences.

Because affirming experiences complemented those that challenged students musically and culturally, Mr. Mitchell's students appeared to view learning as an additive rather than a replacement process. His instruction emphasized systematic style shifting, a process through which students could learn to navigate musical opportunity structures (e.g., audition requirements to demonstrate *bel canto* technique) while retaining expressive contact with their culture of origin. Mr. Mitchell's CRT may therefore have assured students that in broadening their horizons as vocalists, they were not being asked to compromise aspects of their cultural identities.

Fostering Sociopolitical Consciousness

Mr. Mitchell's efforts to promote students' sociopolitical consciousness comprised a salient dimension of his culturally responsive practice. When students expressed concerns about racism and police violence in their community, he designed learning experiences around historically significant repertoire drawn from the United States civil rights movement and the South African anti-apartheid movement. One key example was the South African anti-apartheid piece, *"Thula Sizwe,"* which all three students cited as an example of instruction they perceived to be culturally responsive. Mr. Mitchell supposed this was because the piece related to students' lived experiences:

> When kids hear about these kinds of experiences [e.g., the anti-apartheid and civil rights movements], they actually think even of their own neighborhoods. One actually did say, "Well, that kind of reminds me, even though we're not fighting in the same way that they were, we have a lot of gang activity in our neighborhoods. Sometimes I wonder, how do we make a difference? We can take these messages of empowerment and spread them to the neighborhood and maybe it might touch somebody, maybe it might change someone's mind. I don't really know sometimes if music can do it, but you know, it has to start somewhere, doesn't it?"
>
> Of course, there was that sense of skepticism too: "Will this really work?" . . . not just being so rainbows and smiles about it. They really are considering the pros, the cons, the good, the bad, and saying that,

in spite of it all, something still needs to be said, and we can say something. We can try something instead of just sitting back. . . . Through
music, we can lift our voices and encourage other people to think differently. . . . I think they believe, "I can be the catalyst for change."

Inspired by the notion that their performances "might change someone's
mind" by prompting audiences to think differently, students in the South
Side Choir perceived singing songs of resistance (e.g., "Thula Sizwe," "Ain't
Gonna Let Nobody Turn Me 'Round") to be among their most culturally
responsive experiences. Joyce (2003) explicated the potential for such songs
to effect social change:

> They serve as a point of resistance by speaking the unspeakable or expos-
> ing a reality that is otherwise suppressed and hidden from view. In this
> sense the songs and the singers themselves provide a "voice" for those
> who struggle against oppressive conditions. This has the potential to
> bring comfort and solidarity among those groups who share that expe-
> rience. . . . By listening to these songs, people outside an experience
> can become involved to some extent with the material, thus moving
> people to see differently those experiences of the oppressed that they
> might otherwise be inured to or shielded from. This phenomenon has
> the potential to support or initiate understanding and the building of
> coalitions for social change.
>
> (p. 255)

Her observations align with Mr. Mitchell's belief that "through music, we
can lift our voices and encourage other people to think differently." While
recognizing the potential relevance of such repertoire and experiences, teachers are cautioned against representing any social or cultural group exclusively
through the lens of oppression.

Through pieces such as "Thula Sizwe," Mr. Mitchell opened dialogue
with students about sociopolitical issues, a process through which students began to explore the potential for musical involvement to open avenues for social action. His efforts to promote sociopolitical consciousness
revolved primarily around classroom dialogue and performing repertoire
that invited their audiences' engagement with social issues. While these
efforts are laudable, possibilities for developing students' sociopolitical consciousness extend beyond classroom dialogue and performances aimed at
raising awareness of social issues. As one example, both Zoey and Jazmin
composed music in their free time, a process through which they frequently commented on social issues salient in the community context in
which they lived. They turned to music composition to express "what
goes on in the world" and "things that are and are not right in life." They
were eager to use composition as a vehicle for social commentary, potential
that remained unexplored by their teacher. Possibilities for using creative

engagements such as musical composition as an avenue for CRT, as well as additional options for developing students' sociopolitical consciousness, are discussed in Chapter 6.

Note

1. Trayvon Martin, an unarmed African American 17-year-old, was fatally shot by neighborhood watch volunteer George Zimmerman in 2012. Martin's death, and Zimmerman's acquittal of second-degree murder charges in 2013, sparked outrage and protests in the United States.

References

Bradley, D. (2006). *Global song, global citizens? Multicultural choral music education and the community youth choir: Constituting the multicultural human subject* (Doctoral dissertation). Retrieved from ProQuest Dissertations & Theses. (AAT NR16043).

Burnim, M. V., & Maultsby, P. (1987). From backwoods to city streets: The Afro-American musical journey. In G. Gay & W. Baber (Eds.), *Expressively black: The cultural basis of ethnic identity* (pp. 109–136). New York, NY: Praeger.

Carlow, R. (2004). *Hearing others' voices: An exploration of the music experience of immigrant students who sing in high school choir* (Doctoral dissertation). Retrieved from ProQuest Dissertations & Theses. (AAT 3152852).

Chinn, B. J. (1997). Vocal self-identification, singing style, and singing range in relationship to a measure of cultural mistrust in African-American adolescent females. *Journal of Research in Music Education, 45*(4), 636–649. https://doi.org/10.2307/3345428

Delpit, L. D. (1995). *Other people's children: Cultural conflict in the classroom.* New York, NY: Norton.

Gay, G. (2002). Preparing for culturally responsive teaching. *Journal of Teacher Education, 53*(2), 106–116.

Haskell, J. A. (1987). Vocal self-perception: The other side of the equation. *Journal of Voice, 1*(2), 172–179.

Joyce, V. M. (2003). *Bodies that sing: The formation of singing subjects* (Doctoral dissertation). Retrieved from ProQuest Dissertations & Theses. (AAT NQ78458).

Karlsen, S. (2013). Immigrant students and the "homeland music": Meanings, negotiations, and implications. *Research Studies in Music Education, 35*(2), 161–177. https://doi.org/10.1177/1321103X13508057

Kelly-McHale, J. (2011). *The relationship between children's musical identities and music teacher beliefs and practices in an elementary general music classroom* (Doctoral dissertation). Retrieved from ProQuest Dissertations & Theses. (AAT 3456672).

Killian, J. (1990). Effect of model characteristics on musical preference of junior high school students. *Journal of Research in Music Education, 38*(2), 115–123.

Ladson-Billings, G. J. (1994). *The dream-keepers: Successful teachers of African American children.* San Francisco, CA: Jossey-Bass.

Ladson-Billings, G. J. (2002). I ain't writin' nuttin': Permissions to fail and demands to succeed in urban classrooms. In L. D. Delpit & J. K. Dowdy (Eds.), *The skin that we speak: Thoughts on language and culture in the classroom* (pp. 107–120). New York, NY: Norton.

McCrary, J. (1993). Effects of listeners' and performers' race on music preferences. *Journal of Research in Music Education, 41*(3), 200–211.

McCrary, J. (2000). Ethnic majority/minority status: Children's interactions and affective responses to music. *Journal of Research in Music Education, 48*(3), 249–261. https://doi.org/10.2307/3345397

McCrary, J., & Gauthier, D. (1995). The effects of performers' ethnic identities on pre-adolescents' music preferences. *Update: Applications of Research in Music Education, 14*(1), 20–22.

Morrison, S. J. (1998). A comparison of preference responses of white and African American students to musical versus musical/visual stimuli. *Journal of Research in Music Education, 46*(2), 208–222.

Olneck, M. R. (2004). Immigrants and education in the United States. In J. A. Banks & C. A. M. Banks (Eds.), *Handbook of research on multicultural education* (2nd ed., pp. 381–403). San Francisco, CA: Jossey-Bass.

Rohan, T. J. (2011). *Teaching music, learning culture: The challenge of culturally responsive music education* (Doctoral dissertation). Retrieved from http://hdl.handle.net/10523/1865

Root, M. P. (2004). Multiracial families and children: Implications for educational research and practice. In J. A. Banks & C. A. M. Banks (Eds.), *Handbook of research on multicultural education* (2nd ed.). San Francisco, CA: Jossey-Bass.

Shaw, J. T. (2018). Pedagogical context knowledge: Revelations from a week in the life of itinerant urban music educators. *Music Education Research, 20*(2), 184–200. https://doi.org/10.1080/14613808.2016.1238062

Suárez-Orozco, C., Suárez-Orozco, M. M., & Doucet, F. (2004). The academic engagement and achievement of Latino youth. In J. A. Banks & C. A. M. Banks (Eds.), *Handbook of research on multicultural education* (2nd ed., pp. 420–440). San Francisco, CA: Jossey-Bass.

Suárez-Orozco, C., Suárez-Orozco, M. M., & Todorova, I. (2008). *Learning a new land: Immigrant students in American society* (1st ed.). Cambridge, MA: Harvard University Press.

Thibeault, M. D. (2009). The violin and the fiddle: Narratives of music and musician in a high-school setting. In C. R. Abril & J. L. Kerchner (Eds.), *Musical experience in our lives: Things we learn and meanings we make* (pp. 255–276). Lanham, MD: Rowman & Littlefield.

Walker, L. B. (2006). Influence of musical characteristics on style preferences of African American students in urban areas. *Bulletin of the Council for Research in Music Education, 168*, 7–19.

Ward-Steinman, P. M. (2006). The development of an after-school music program for at-risk children: Student musical preferences and pre-service teacher reflections. *International Journal of Music Education, 24*(1), 85–96.

5 Lessons Learned From Students' Experiences Across the Three Choirs

The preceding chapters presented portraits of culturally responsive choral music education as practiced in three demographically contrasting communities, highlighting themes distinctive to each choir. This chapter describes overarching themes that were salient across the three choir sites, highlighting students' perspectives on learning experiences they considered, or did not consider, to be culturally responsive. A first set of themes crystallizes elements of instruction students in all three choirs perceived to be culturally responsive. A second set of themes reveals potential barriers to CRT illuminated by singers' accounts of their experiences.

Instruction Students Perceived to Be Culturally Responsive

Several themes emerged from students' descriptions of instruction they considered culturally responsive: developing cultural competence while expanding cultural horizons, attending to cultural validity, and developing an ability to style shift.

Developing Cultural Competence While Expanding Students' Horizons

Students valued teachers' efforts to engage them in musical experiences that helped them better understand and appreciate their own cultural backgrounds and identities. These opportunities corresponded with Ladson-Billings' (2002) notion of developing "cultural competence" (p. 111). This theme was prevalent in the West Side Choir, where Mr. Moses intentionally sought correspondence between musical experiences he planned for his choirs and the cultural identities of specific individuals. For instance, students performed selections from Argentina, Colombia, Chile, Puerto Rico, and Venezuela within a single concert, with each of these musical traditions bearing a direct connection to at least one student's lived experiences. Kristina described these opportunities as motivating, Shirin described them as fostering a sense of pride, and Mateo perceived them to be affirming on a visceral level. In the

South Side Choir, learning experiences that fostered cultural competence for Zoey and Jazmin included those featuring culturally relevant vocal models. Describing opportunities to learn choral literature relevant to her Puerto Rican heritage, North Side singer Daniella shared, "I appreciate that, just knowing my teacher respects and knows about my culture."

While students valued learning opportunities that honored their cultural heritages and affirmed their cultural identities, they desired additional experiences that would challenge them beyond the realm of their prior knowledge and experiences. Students' perspectives aligned with assertions of leading theorists, who have emphasized that CRT must broaden students' horizons as much as it validates their own backgrounds (e.g., Gay, 2002; Ladson-Billings, 1994; Villegas & Lucas, 2002). Teachers will ideally balance learning experiences that productively challenge students with those that build on cultural assets they bring to the choral classroom, taking care not to position any cultural or musical tradition as more valid than another.

Attending to Cultural Validity

Across choir sites, teachers and students emphasized the critical importance of cultural validity to developing learning experiences students will receive as being culturally responsive. Attending to cultural validity entails thoroughly researching details pertaining to performance practice, vocal timbre and style, pronunciation, physical movement, instrumentation, pedagogical approach, and performance venues; striving for the most faithful and accurate representation of each culture possible. Additionally, teacher-conductors must take responsibility for thoroughly understanding the piece's historical, social, cultural, and political context and presenting such information accurately to the choir.

As one example of a misguided approach to CRT, music educators may integrate repertoire drawn from diverse cultural traditions into their curricula, but present every piece through a Eurocentric pedagogical lens regardless of its culture of origin. Applying discourse norms associated with Western classical music within inappropriate cultural contexts can result in experiences that are confusing, alienating, or offensive to students who identify with the culture supposedly being represented. For example, Mr. Mitchell related that hearing African American spirituals performed with a characteristically Western European vocal timbre and inappropriate performance practices "makes you cringe in your seat, especially as an African American, when you hear these songs, your heritage, being sung in such a way." Sarah described the importance of performing music representing her Korean heritage in as culturally valid a manner as possible: "I get more protective over the song. When we mess up, I take it more personally. . . . I get upset." Comments such as Sarah's and Mr. Mitchell's illuminate the potential for learning experiences to be alienating rather than affirming if teachers do not thoroughly attend to issues of cultural validity.

All three teachers went to great efforts to ensure the cultural validity of learning experiences, which students noted and valued. They emphasized singing with accurate pronunciation, vocal timbre and style, physical movement, and additional performance practices appropriate for each piece studied. Further, teachers made conscious, informed decisions to teach orally or from a notated score depending on how that music would be learned within its culture of origin. Consulting with culture bearers, or representatives of each culture studied (Campbell, 2004), was one strategy conductors used to maximize cultural validity. In some cases, members of students' families served as culture bearers, a practice that drew upon families' "funds of knowledge" to meaningfully instruct students (see Moll & González, 2004).

Style Shifting: Musical Code-Switching

Students in all three choirs experienced singing with a diverse array of vocal timbres, styles, and performance practices, each appropriate to the cultural tradition represented. Rather than asserting that any particular vocal style or timbre was correct in an absolute sense, teachers guided students to discover the musical situations for which each was appropriate. As a result of these experiences, singers developed an ability to fluidly navigate between vocal styles appropriate to a variety of culturally and stylistically diverse repertoire. This ability to style shift resembles the sociolinguistic concept of "code-switching" which refers to "systematic shifting or alternation between languages" (Grant & Ladson-Billings, 1997, p. 44).

Within choral music education, an ability to sing with Western European vocal timbre and *bel canto* technique often serves as advantageous cultural capital for being promoted within choral organizations or gaining entrance into ensembles in the first place. Mr. Moses, Ms. Rose, and Mr. Mitchell provided opportunities for students to develop these skills while continuing to showcase additional performance styles with which students were skilled. Equipping students to navigate a "culture of power" without asserting the superiority of knowledge and skills holding privileged positions is one way that teachers can convey an affirming attitude toward culturally diverse learners (Villegas & Lucas, 2002). Style shifting provided a way for students to navigate musical opportunity structures while continuing to express themselves musically in ways that aligned with their cultural identities.

Potential Barriers to CRT Illuminated by Students' Experiences

Students' perceptions of learning experiences they considered to be culturally responsive, as previously described, can be informative to teachers as they make important curricular and pedagogical decisions. Equally informative are students' descriptions of experiences they did not perceive to be culturally responsive, despite teachers' well-intentioned efforts. The following section presents cross-case themes that illuminate potential barriers to CRT. Identifying and discussing these potential barriers to CRT is not intended to suggest that they are insurmountable. Rather, by recognizing and proactively anticipating potential barriers, teachers can take conscious action toward ameliorating them.

Limiting Culturally Responsive Practice to Content Integration

The culturally responsive practice of all three teachers focused primarily on having students learn and perform choral repertoire representing diverse cultural traditions, recreating these traditions in as culturally valid a manner as possible. It is important to recognize that including repertoire representing diverse cultural traditions in the curriculum, while an important preliminary step, does not in and of itself constitute CRT. Thoroughly infusing one's curriculum with diverse content and perspectives, including but not limited to repertoire, is but one of many components of CRT identified by leading authors in the field (see Gay, 2002, 2010; Ladson-Billings, 1994, 1995; McKoy & Lind, 2016; Villegas & Lucas, 2002). Further, substitutions in content may do little to alter curricula that remain Eurocentric at their core.

As the North Side Choir case illustrated, content integration can occur independently of considerations of the specific learners to whom CRT is intended to respond, undermining the student-centered premises that distinguish this approach to teaching. Additionally, teacher-student relationships in culturally responsive classrooms are characterized by a spirit of reciprocity in which each learns from the other. When teachers assume primary or exclusive responsibility for selecting repertoire on students' behalf, it is all too easy to miss opportunities to learn from students about repertoire and experiences they consider to be culturally relevant.

Further, approaching multicultural or culturally responsive choral music education primarily by singing repertoire representing diverse cultural traditions does not go far enough toward the transformation or social action approaches advocated by authors such as Banks (2005), which aim for complete transformation of hegemonic instructional structures. An important dimension of CRT involves helping students develop the critical capacities to recognize and challenge hegemonic structures that disproportionately limit the educational opportunities of students from nondominant communities. It is entirely possible for students to learn repertoire representing diverse cultural traditions, even in a way that accurately and faithfully represents the cultures from which the repertoire originates, without engaging in the type of critical dialogue or analysis necessary to recognize oppressive conditions or take action toward social change. Teachers are then encouraged to go beyond content integration, giving balanced attention to additional dimensions of CRT. They might especially emphasize elements aimed at developing students' critical capacities such as Ladson-Billings' (2002) concept of developing sociopolitical consciousness and Villegas and Lucas's (2002) recommendation to engage students in inquiry projects calling for students' critical analyses of and action toward addressing social issues.

Students' Perceptions of Crossing Style Parameters

From a comparative analysis of students' experiences with CRT across the three choirs, one salient finding was that Zoey and Jazmin explicitly equated some terms of engagement with a "White" way of singing. These included the Western classical canon; notation-based learning strategies; and the timbre, tone, and vocal style associated with Western European singing. Additionally, they were the only two singers to directly discuss hesitation or resistance toward emulating what they perceived to be White vocal models. They expressed a preference for singing with their "regular voices," which involved extensive use of chest voice, a comfortably low vocal range, and freedom to apply stylistic qualities associated with African American singing such as bends, glides, hard vocal attacks, and raspiness (see Burnim & Maultsby, 1987; Chinn, 1997).

Scholars have suggested that the historical and political circumstances surrounding how cultural groups became part of U.S. society hold consequences for students' orientations toward and engagement in education. One potentially informative distinction is that between groups who voluntarily became a part of U.S. society, as through migration or immigration, and those that were incorporated involuntarily, as through colonization or slavery. Ogbu and Simons (1998) posited that voluntary and involuntary minorities may differ in terms of "symbolic response," or how they "understand and interpret the differences between their culture and language and White American culture and language" (p. 174). They explained:

> Crossing cultural/language boundaries has a very different meaning for voluntary and involuntary minorities. . . . Involuntary minorities [may] interpret the cultural and language differences as markers of collective identity to be maintained, not merely barriers to be overcome. In responding to their forced incorporation into U.S. society and subsequent mistreatment, they develop a collective identity defined to a great extent by its difference from and opposition to White American identity. Given this interpretation, some individuals feel that if they learn White American ways or "White talk" they will lose their [cultural] identity. For them, adopting White ways and language is a subtractive or replacement process that . . . therefore is resisted.
>
> (pp. 174–175)

While scholars have subsequently extended and critiqued aspects of this theory (see, for example, Gibson, 1997; Goldenberg, 2014), the possibility that students might associate specific musical traditions, pieces, or vocal performance practices with present or generational experiences of oppression merits teachers' attention.

In light of considerations such as these, an approach to teaching that treats acquiring new knowledge and skills as a subtractive or replacement process serves as a potential barrier to CRT. This barrier can appear in choral music education when teachers insist that there is only one "correct" way to sing and expect singers to sacrifice culturally preferred ways of singing in order to embrace a tradition positioned as "more legitimate." Teachers can ameliorate this potential barrier by respecting students' preferred ways of engaging with music as being valid and valuable even as they challenge them toward new learning. They can recognize that students' preferred vocal styles may function as expressions of collective identity with cultural communities to which they belong and open spaces for students to express themselves in these ways. Further, teachers can encourage students to view expanding their musical capabilities as an additive, rather than a replacement, process. Villegas and Lucas (2002) emphasized that viewing the teacher's role "as adding to rather than replacing what students bring to learning" is important to maintaining an affirming attitude toward culturally diverse learners (p. 23).

Decontextualized Learning Experiences

Insufficient attention to historical, social, cultural, and political context in the teaching and learning process presents another potential barrier to CRT. This barrier tends to arise when teachers are myopically focused on musical aspects of instruction to the extent that additional contextual details are overlooked. An exchange with Jazmin illustrates how neglecting to fully contextualize a musical experience can result in incomplete understandings of cultural and musical traditions studied:

Julia: Did you learn any songs from cultures with which you were not familiar?

Jazmin: "*Shalom Chaverim*." I don't know what country it's from. He didn't tell me that.

Julia: Well, "*Shalom Chaverim*" is sung in Hebrew and relates to Jewish culture. Have you met any Jewish people before?

Jazmin: Yeah, one time we went to see my auntie and there were a lot of people speaking in a different language. She told me that they were Jewish and I was like, "What?"

Julia: Did singing "*Shalom Chaverim*" make you think any differently about Jewish people?

Jazmin: Well, it made me think that they didn't have to go through what we went through. They probably didn't know about it, or read articles about it, but never felt it before.

By "what we went through," Jazmin meant African Americans' experiences of oppression, racism, and prejudice in American society. She assumed that Jewish people had not encountered similarly oppressive experiences. I asked

Jazmin if she had ever learned about the Holocaust in choir or school, and she confirmed that she had not.

This exchange demonstrates that experiencing a single piece of choral literature was insufficient for developing Jazmin's knowledge about Jewish culture. Although she had experienced singing *"Shalom Chaverim"* in choir, she could not name the language in which it was sung, explain the song's meaning, or identify a sociocultural group for whom the song might hold meaning. Her comments illustrate that an isolated, decontextualized encounter with choral repertoire will not in and of itself accomplish CRT's broader goals, such as promoting intercultural understanding or fostering thoughtful valuation of previously unfamiliar cultural traditions.

Kelly-McHale (2018) further emphasized the importance of understanding and accurately teaching contextual details surrounding repertoire choices in a column tracing the historical roots of "Jump Jim Crow/Joe." This song gained entrance into the accepted canon of elementary music repertoire despite its historic roots in blackface minstrelsy during the Jim Crow era. As Kelly-McHale explained, the character Jim Crow "became a tool for marginalization by White people who desired to create the notion that African slaves were content and happy with their lives, and it became a staple of the minstrel shows that continued through the early twentieth century" (p. 61). Music teachers unaware of this piece's history might perceive it as a "fun" or "catchy" song with an enjoyable dance, and could unwittingly facilitate deeply offensive classroom experiences for students who are aware of the song's contextual implications.

Parallels exist within choral music education when genres such as African American spirituals and South African anti-apartheid songs, to name but two examples, are presented in ways that gloss over oppressive circumstances surrounding their creation (see Sieck, 2017 for detailed treatment of these issues). It is incumbent upon teachers to thoroughly research and accurately present the historical, cultural, social, and political context surrounding any piece their choir will study or perform, a process that requires delving deeper than consulting information provided in the inside cover of an octavo. For pieces with historic roots in oppressive circumstances, teachers can determine a plan for ethically addressing those contextual details with students or seek an alternative piece that serves the same instructional goals.

Hierarchical Views of Musical Value

Comparing students' perceptions of sociocultural discourse norms across choir sites revealed an additional barrier to cultural responsiveness: a hierarchical orientation that upholds the Western classical canon and its associated pedagogical discourses as the most legitimate to study and perform, even as additional traditions are included in the curriculum. In the North Side Choir, an additive approach to curriculum integration, in which the curriculum remained Eurocentric at its core, contributed toward students' perceptions that Western classical music was the most legitimate to study and perform. There, the predominance of discourse norms associated with Western classical singing contributed to two related student perceptions: that reading music from notation was superior to learning music aurally, and that the timbre, tone, and vocal style associated with Western European singing was a golden standard for "excellent singing." These discourse norms influenced the ways students evaluated their success and whether they self-identified as musicians or singers.

These students' perceptions exemplify how a hierarchical view of the value or legitimacy of particular genres and their associated pedagogic discourses presents a potential barrier to CRT. Therefore, a foundational step toward CRT involves developing conscious awareness of messages communicated to students about the kinds of musicians and musical experiences that are valued within our classrooms (Lamont & Maton, 2010; Rohan, 2011). Following is a list of considerations and guiding questions intended to prompt teachers' reflection on aspects of choral pedagogy that can convey messages about musical value to students, whether explicitly or implicitly.

Composition of the Curriculum

The relative number of learning experiences representing particular cultural or musical traditions within a given academic year or performance season can convey messages about the value of those traditions. Teachers might then reflect on questions such as the following:

- Is the curriculum thoroughly infused with diverse content and perspectives? Or are encounters with music representing diverse cultures treated as "add-ons" to a curriculum that remains Eurocentric at its core?
- Are opportunities to learn music drawn from diverse musical traditions limited to single, isolated encounters?
- Are there opportunities to delve deeply into learning about a specific culture by learning several selections from that culture?

Repertoire-Related Decisions

Repertoire serves as a prominent vehicle for delivering the curriculum within choral classrooms, making teachers' repertoire-related decisions a source of messages about musical value. Lists of sanctioned, recommended, or approved repertoire compiled by state music associations or professional organizations often influence teachers' repertoire-related decision making. While these lists are potential sources of educationally sound suggestions, it is important to recognize that they are not neutral, but reflect particular cultural perspectives and values. As a case in point, an article published in the *Choral Journal* (Watson, 2017) provided a compilation of titles that appeared most frequently on high school state choral festival lists. The article drew a response from the American Choral Directors Association's Diversity Initiatives Committee (Amrein & Diversity Initiatives Committee, 2017) noting that the lists were dominated by male composers (204 of 208 selections), composers from North American and Europe (203 of 208), Caucasian composers (194 of 208), and sacred texts from the Christian tradition (136 of 136).

Students are keenly aware of whether and how sociocultural groups with which they identify are represented in curricular materials including repertoire. Considering this, teachers might reflect on questions such as the following:

- How are people belonging to social groups relating to age, gender, race, ethnicity, socioeconomic status, sexual orientation, and exceptionality represented (or not represented) in repertoire?
- In what ways can the curriculum be more thoroughly infused with content and perspectives that respectfully represent those groups?
- Do students study works by composers representing a diverse range of cultural identities?
- Are pieces selected for study and performance mostly drawn from the Western classical canon?
- Are selections representative of diverse cultural groups each treated with substantial emphasis?
- In what ways are my repertoire-related decisions informed by lists of approved large group adjudicated event literature? Have I taken care to include works contributed by groups that have historically been under-represented or absent from these lists?

Instructional Time and Seriousness of Purpose

Students also draw conclusions about musical value from how the teacher allocates instructional time and the seriousness with which they approach teaching various musical and cultural traditions. Questions such as the following then merit consideration:

- How much time is devoted to rehearsing selections drawn from each musical and cultural tradition explored?
- Are certain selections routinely relegated to the last five minutes of rehearsal, while others are afforded greater amounts of rehearsal time when students are most mentally fresh and alert?
- Does the teacher's demeanor change when rehearsing a specific genre, contributing a different degree of seriousness of purpose or intensity to the experience?
- Is the conductor equally attentive to detail with each selection rehearsed, or are some pieces given only a surface-level treatment?
- Has the conductor undertaken an equally intensive process of preparing each selection, or do some pieces or genres receive the bulk of the conductor's "score study" attention?

Role Models

From the musical role models we uphold in the classroom, students envision (or fail to envision) future possibilities for themselves as professionals or aficionados within the field of choral music. Accordingly, teachers can consider questions such as the following:

- Are musicians representing diverse cultural backgrounds upheld as role models for students to emulate?
- Do students receive opportunities to interact with guest performers, conductors, or clinicians who share the same race, ethnicity, gender, and additional salient facets of identity?
- Are musicians from diverse cultural groups represented in the symbolic curriculum, including posters, images, bulletin boards, awards, and the like? Or do these materials primarily reflect the images of dominant or privileged social groups?

Vocal Models

Educators can further consider the vocal models upheld for students to emulate, reflecting on questions such as the following:

- Are diverse vocal models presented as a desirable standard of singing to which students can aspire?
- How do we describe what constitutes an ideal choral sound?
- Is one style of singing positioned as the most or only correct way to sing, or do students explore multiple, valid approaches to singing and the contexts for which they are appropriate?

Teachers sometimes express hesitancy to approach unfamiliar vocal timbres out of concern for students' vocal health. Let us ensure that such concerns are not driven by assumptions or personal biases about what types of music are "appropriate" or "legitimate" to study. One question for choral teachers' critical self-reflection concerns whether musical contributions of particular sociocultural groups, especially those of people of color, are excluded from the curriculum more frequently than others due to vocal health concerns that may not be well substantiated from a voice science or medical perspective.

Teachers have an obligation to attend to students' vocal health regardless of the musical genre being learned or the culture in which it originated. If students are learning to recreate a vocal timbre beyond the realm of their prior experience, continue to promote healthy vocal technique through attention to matters such as posture, breath support and management, and tension reduction. Respect developing singers' endurance limits as they broach new vocal timbres and styles.

Concert Programming

The presentation of selections within a broader concert program can convey unintended messages about musical value. For example, I once heard a conference presenter explaining the value of "dessert" selections that offer audiences a light and fun experience at the conclusion of a concert. When the audience asked what types of selections make ideal "dessert pieces," the presenter responded, "any multicultural piece." Such a view is problematic when repertoire drawn from diverse cultural traditions is always or only treated as "dessert," as opposed to musical traditions of value that deserve serious, respectful treatment. Further issues arise when serious aspects of a piece's historical, social, cultural, and political context, such as historical roots in violence or oppression, are overlooked in the process of presenting the piece as "dessert." We might then ask ourselves:

- Are pieces representing diverse cultural traditions always or very frequently programmed as the final piece in a concert, contributing to possible impressions that that music drawn from those traditions are *always* or *only* "light and fun"?
- Are pieces drawn from particular traditions treated as "fun" in a way that suggests that they don't merit singers' best efforts?

This discussion is not intended to suggest that learning music representative of any particular cultural tradition cannot be a fun or joyful experience, or that decisions to program particular genres as concert closers are inherently wrong. Rather, teachers are encouraged to consider whether positioning any tradition solely as "light and fun" contributes to students' surface-level understandings of the tradition or misperceptions that the music is not legitimate or valuable.

Organizational Opportunity Structures

Choral teachers can further consider messages sent by the types of knowledge and skills rewarded with opportunity within choral organizations (e.g., progressing to more advanced ensembles, or receiving solos or lead roles). Reflection on the following questions might be informative:

- For what kinds of knowledge, skills, and dispositions are students promoted or rewarded within the choral organization?
- Are discourse norms associated with Western classical music (e.g., an ability to sight-read or to sing with *bel canto* vocal technique) more advantageous for achieving membership in an advanced choir?

By reflecting on areas of choral practice such as those described above, teachers can develop conscious awareness of messages students receive about

musical value and legitimacy and work to develop a classroom environment that conveys respect for multiple, valid ways of engaging with
music.

The Challenge and Opportunity of Responding to Personal Culture

Students identified the complexity involved in determining what music
students consider culturally relevant as presenting a potential implementation challenge to their teachers. The portraits presented in Chapters 2, 3,
and 4 illustrate the multifaceted nature of nine students' cultural identities,
which were shaped by their identifications with social groups defined by
class, race, ethnicity, gender, nationality, religion, sexual orientation, exceptionality, and so on. These variables interacted in complex ways, making
each student's cultural identity individualized and distinctive. Thus, students' experiences illustrate Erickson's (2005) notion of "personal culture."
As he explained:

> Individuals participate in multiple communities of practice, acquiring
> multiple microcultural repertoires as their own personal culture, and
> these repertoires differ from one individual to the next among persons
> with the "same" social category (e.g., class, race, gender). . . . Where
> one shows up, in which local communities of practice and how often,
> provides each individual with opportunities for cultural learning that
> are so distinct, so site specific and person specific, that they are literally
> unique.
>
> (p. 38)

The fact that each human voice is also literally unique is a distinguishing
facet of vocal pedagogy, making choral music education an ideal context for
responding to personal culture on an individual level.

Considering the complex, idiosyncratic, and dynamic nature of cultural
identity, teachers are cautioned against essentializing culture by assuming that
all people belonging to a social category are culturally similar (Erickson,
2005). For example, rather than regarding one's Spanish-speaking students
as one culturally homogenous group, culturally responsive teachers develop
knowledge about the specific ethnic, national, and cultural traditions with
which their specific students identify. For instance, students in this volume
identified as Guatemalan, Honduran, Mexican, and Puerto Rican. Students'
identification with these and additional specific cultural communities holds
implications for the types of learning experiences they will find culturally
relevant.

Ladson-Billings' (1994) term "culture of reference," which refers to the cultural group, including ethnic and racial characteristics, with which one most
identifies, may be useful to teachers in thinking through the complexities

involved in responding pedagogically to students' idiosyncratic cultural identities (p. 28). For example, although Shirin identified with Irish, Persian, African American, and Filipino culture as her cultures of origin, her experiences growing up with a Puerto Rican stepfather in a community with a substantial Puerto Rican migrant population led her to identify with Puerto Rican culture as a culture of reference. When planning instruction, teachers are advised to consider that students' cultures of reference may not correspond with their cultures of origin and that they may identify with multiple cultures.

Practicing CRT effectively therefore involves guarding against making assumptions about students' cultural identities or the experiences they will consider culturally relevant. As Karlsen (2013) emphasized:

> Students' identities—their individual, social, cultural, and musical selves—are most likely multifaceted, plural, complex and even contradictory . . . these students also have the right to be recognized, acknowledged and respected as such, without teachers jumping to conclusions and defining their selves on their behalf.
>
> (p. 172)

Further complicating matters for music teachers who desire to practice CRT is the notion that students' cultural and musical identities may not correspond in predictable ways. As Shirin's and Delores's cases exemplified, students themselves may not be able to readily identify what repertoire or musical experiences might constitute CRT for them.

This raises the question of how teachers can identify an appropriate point of departure for engaging students through CRT. One seemingly obvious answer is to respectfully inquire about students' cultural backgrounds, identities, and life experiences. Questionnaires, journaling, autobiographical assignments, icebreaker activities, and informal conversations with students may yield insight into experiences students will find culturally relevant. Gay's (2002) first essential element of CRT, developing a knowledge base about cultural diversity, then comes into play. Having learned from students about experiences they would consider culturally relevant, teachers must then continually invest effort into deepening their knowledge of the specific cultural communities with which students identify.

Because CRT evolves through an interactive process characterized by the teacher's *response* to students' cultural identities and lived experiences, understanding students' experiences and perspectives is essential to practicing it well. Accordingly, this chapter presented prominent themes in students' accounts of instruction they considered, or did not consider, to be culturally responsive. The following chapter explores practical implications of these themes, offering recommendations for teacher-conductors interested in practicing culturally responsive choral pedagogy.

References

Amrein, E., & Diversity Initiatives Committee. (2017). Letter to the editor. *Choral Journal, 58*(4), 6.

Banks, J. A. (2005). Approaches to multicultural curriculum reform. In J. A. Banks & C. A. M. Banks (Eds.), *Multicultural education: Issues and perspectives* (5th ed., pp. 242–261). Hoboken, NJ: Wiley.

Burnim, M. V., & Maultsby, P. (1987). From backwoods to city streets: The Afro-American musical journey. In G. Gay & W. Baber (Eds.), *Expressively black: The cultural basis of ethnic identity* (pp. 109–136). New York, NY: Praeger.

Campbell, P. S. (2004). *Teaching music globally: Experiencing music, expressing culture.* New York, NY: Oxford University Press.

Chinn, B. J. (1997). Vocal self-identification, singing style, and singing range in relationship to a measure of cultural mistrust in African-American adolescent females. *Journal of Research in Music Education, 45*(4), 636–649. https://doi.org/10.2307/3345428

Erickson, F. (2005). Culture in society and in educational practices. In J. A. Banks & C. A. M. Banks (Eds.), *Multicultural education: Issues and perspectives* (5th ed., pp. 31–60). Hoboken, NJ: Wiley.

Gay, G. (2002). Preparing for culturally responsive teaching. *Journal of Teacher Education, 53*(2), 106–116.

Gay, G. (2010). *Culturally responsive teaching: Theory, research, and practice* (2nd ed.). New York, NY: Teachers College Press.

Gibson, M. A. (1997). Complicating the immigrant/involuntary minority typology. *Anthropology and Education Quarterly, 28*(3), 431–454.

Goldenberg, B. M. (2014). White teachers in urban classrooms: Embracing non-white students' cultural capital for better teaching and learning. *Urban Education, 49*(1), 111–144. https://doi.org/10.1177/0042085912472510

Grant, C. A., & Ladson-Billings, G. J. (1997). *Dictionary of multicultural education.* Phoenix, AZ: Oryz Press.

Karlsen, S. (2013). Immigrant students and the "homeland music": Meanings, negotiations, and implications. *Research Studies in Music Education, 35*(2), 161–177. https://doi.org/10.1177/1321103X13508057

Kelly-McHale, J. (2018). Equity in music education: Exclusionary practices in music education. *Music Educators Journal, 104*(3), 60–62. https://doi.org/10.1177/0027432117744755

Ladson-Billings, G. J. (1994). *The dream-keepers: Successful teachers of African American children.* San Francisco, CA: Jossey-Bass.

Ladson-Billings, G. J. (1995). Toward a theory of culturally relevant pedagogy. *American Educational Research Journal, 32*(3), 465–491. https://doi.org/10.3102/00028312032003465

Ladson-Billings, G. J. (2002). I ain't writin' nuttin': Permissions to fail and demands to succeed in urban classrooms. In L. D. Delpit & J. K. Dowdy (Eds.), *The skin that we speak: Thoughts on language and culture in the classroom* (pp. 107–120). New York, NY: Norton.

Lamont, A., & Maton, K. (2010). Unpopular music: Beliefs and behaviors toward music in education. In R. Wright (Ed.), *Sociology and music education* (pp. 63–80). Burlington, VT: Ashgate.

McKoy, C. L., & Lind, V. L. (2016). *Culturally responsive teaching in music education: From understanding to application.* New York, NY: Routledge.

Moll, L. C., & González, G. (2004). Engaging life: A funds-of-knowledge approach to multicultural education. In J. A. Banks & C. A. M. Banks (Eds.), *Handbook of research on multicultural education* (2nd ed., pp. 699–715). San Francisco, CA: Jossey-Bass.

Ogbu, J. U., & Simons, H. D. (1998). Voluntary & involuntary minorities: A cross-ecological theory of school performance with some implications for education. *Anthropology and Education Quarterly*, 29(2), 155–188. https://doi.org/10.1525/aeq.1998.29.2.155

Rohan, T. J. (2011). *Teaching music, learning culture: The challenge of culturally responsive music education* (Doctoral dissertation). Retrieved from http://hdl.handle.net/10523/1865

Sieck, S. (2017). *Teaching with respect: Inclusive pedagogy for choral directors.* Milwaukee, WI: Hal Leonard.

Villegas, A. M., & Lucas, T. (2002). Preparing culturally responsive teachers: Rethinking the curriculum. *Journal of Teacher Education, 53*(1), 20–32. https://doi.org/10.1177/0022487102053001003

Watson, J. (2017). Most recommended choral music from 20 state music lists. *Choral Journal, 58*(2), 8–23.

6 Recommendations and Future Possibilities

This book has described how three teachers of differing ethnicities practiced CRT in demographically contrasting classrooms, as well as how nine students received the resulting learning experiences. Collectively, their portraits highlight a range of pedagogical possibilities for responding to cultural diversity through choral pedagogy. This chapter explores practical implications of themes that emerged from students' accounts of their experiences, offering recommendations for choral music educators who seek to practice CRT.

CRT is an approach to teaching rather than a prescriptive method. There is no single curriculum design, instructional plan, collection of repertoire, or set of recommendations that can guarantee culturally responsive practice for teachers in any context. Teachers' approaches to CRT will ideally be personalized for each learner, and its practice will unfold differently in each educational context. This chapter is therefore not intended to offer a prescription or recipe for practicing CRT, but instead offers principles, considerations, and guiding questions intended to be helpful to teachers as they undertake the work of designing CRT with their particular learners.

Reframing the Teacher–Student Relationship

The word *responsive* in "culturally responsive teaching" refers to teachers' responses to students' cultural backgrounds and identities, implying a student-centered approach. CRT is also an asset-based pedagogy, meaning that teachers build on the knowledge, perspectives, experiences, and strengths learners contribute to the classroom community rather than viewing education as a process of remedying supposed deficits. Such a student-centered, asset-based approach to pedagogy requires a reconceptualization of the teacher-conductor's role from "teacher as repository of knowledge" to that of a teacher willing to learn from and alongside students (Abril, 2009, p. 89). The teacher-conductor is frequently positioned the only "expert" in the choral classroom, and too often bears sole responsibility for making artistic decisions and guiding singers to execute their artistic vision as expeditiously as possible. This approach to musical leadership may be appropriate in professional contexts, but merits reframing if the goal is to practice CRT in educational settings.

As Delpit (1995) asserted, "The teacher cannot be the only expert in the classroom. To deny students their own expert knowledge is to disempower them" (p. 32–33). Practicing CRT well therefore requires admitting when we don't hold certain knowledge, being willing to engage in serious study of musical styles and genres with which we may not initially be comfortable, and remaining receptive to what students can teach us about musical experiences they consider culturally relevant. As Mostern (1994) emphasized, "This does not mean that the teacher denies his or her pedagogical intentions or specific expertise, but merely that s/he respects the myriad expertise of the students that s/he does not share" (p. 256).

Designing a Curriculum of Culturally Responsive Experiences

Developing a well-coordinated curriculum of learning experiences that are informed by and responsive to cultural diversity is foundational to culturally responsive practice. Rather than approaching curriculum design from a repertoire-centered (Carlow, 2004), "score-centered" (Thibeault, 2009) or "sequence-centered" perspective (Kelly-McHale, 2011), culturally responsive educators place students at the center of the curriculum.

Balancing Affirming and Broadening Experiences

Leading theorists have explained that CRT must expand students' horizons as much as it validates their own cultural backgrounds and identities (Gay, 2002; Ladson-Billings, 1994; Villegas & Lucas, 2002), a perspective student contributors to this book shared. As I have previously suggested, envisioning a continuum ranging from "cultural validation" of students' own backgrounds to "thoughtful valuation" of less culturally familiar music may be helpful to teachers as they design a curriculum of culturally responsive learning experiences. In this model,

> teachers plan experiences that provide students with cultural valida-
> tion, then help students progress toward thoughtfully valuing music that
> has previously been beyond the realm of their personal experiences.
> "Thoughtful valuation," a term borrowed from Dewey (1925, p. 437)
> that refers to mediation and criticism of experience, reflects an ultimate
> aim of culturally responsive teaching. . . . Students should go beyond
> mere exposure to, familiarity with, or passive acceptance of music rep-
> resentative of diverse cultures, learning to value it with thoughtfulness,
> intelligence, and a sense of social responsibility.
>
> (Shaw, 2012, p. 79)

Figure 6.1 Culturally Responsive Curriculum Continuum

Source: © 2012 by National Association for Music Education (formerly MENC). Reprinted with permission.

Note: Figure from Shaw, J. T. (2012). The skin that we sing: Culturally responsive choral music education. *Music Educators Journal*, 98(4), 75–81.

This model is not intended to suggest that any type of music students encounter along that continuum is more valuable or legitimate than another. Sequencing culturally validating experiences prior to those that productively challenge students may, however, present pedagogical advantages. Culturally validating experiences might convey to students that their cultural knowledge is valued within the choral organization, allow rapport and trust to develop between teacher and student, and bolster students' confidence and self-efficacy. Such experiences might support students' openness toward subsequent learning experiences that are more challenging, less familiar, or initially less comfortable. However, this does not mean that the music students consider culturally relevant should be used only in service to the goal of eventually learning Western classical music or any genre deemed "more legitimate" to study or perform.

Defining the Curriculum's Scope

Rather than facilitating isolated encounters with single selections drawn from a large number of cultural traditions, teachers might choose to present multiple selections from selected "cultures of emphasis" for in-depth exploration. Presenting fewer cultural traditions in greater depth, whether within a single concert cycle or across an academic year, can support educators' thorough preparation to teach those traditions. Focusing on a practically manageable number of cultural traditions also helps teachers allocate sufficient instructional time for students to master new skills (e.g., accurate pronunciation of unfamiliar languages, recreation of less-familiar vocal timbres, successful incorporation of recently learned performance practices) and develop deep understanding of contextual detail. By strategically defining the curriculum's scope, teachers can promote substantive engagement with each culture studied and increase the likelihood that students' performances will be received as culturally valid and respectful.

Identifying a Point of Departure

Given the vast number of cultural and musical traditions available for classroom exploration, teachers may be challenged to identify an appropriate point of departure for practicing CRT. Following are some suggestions for selecting a cultural tradition with which to begin:

- Start with a musical and cultural tradition about which you are knowledgeable and feel well-prepared to teach.
- Develop an autobiographical lesson based on music that you consider relevant to your own cultural identity. Invite students to contribute examples of music that function similarly in their lives. For example, having taught a lullaby that holds significance within your family, invite students to provide examples of music that similarly helps them relax. Having taught a dance relevant to your own cultural background, ask students about occasions on which they dance and the types of music that support those experiences. Students' responses will likely suggest directions for future lessons. Use repertoire students bring to the classroom as the basis for an inquiry project, as inspiration for a composition activity, or as performance literature for your ensemble.
- Music relevant to a classroom majority group, or a group with a significant cultural presence in the school or community, may present a logical point of departure for CRT. As Gianna's experience illustrated, care must be taken to balance experiences that are responsive to a classroom majority group with attention to and opportunities for students who do not identify with that group.
- A cultural tradition with which students are likely to be equally unfamiliar could provide a productive point of departure in that students may be equally challenged by the experience.
- A school-wide focus on a specific culture, or a culture emphasized in students' coursework outside of music, could inform music teachers' decisions to emphasize that culture.
- Capitalize on the cultural richness found within your school's community as a point of departure for CRT. Inquire about musical and cultural expertise held by students' families, teacher colleagues in the school, members of nearby community organizations, and so forth.

Experiences That Broaden Students' Horizons

Broadening students' horizons might involve a degree of personal discomfort as they acquire knowledge and skills beyond the realm of their prior experience. It is therefore essential to attend to students' dispositions and self-efficacy as they engage in experiences that challenge them. Following are some recommendations for designing learning experiences that broaden students' cultural horizons:

- Consider ways to use cultural scaffolding, drawing upon culturally familiar elements (e.g., a specific rhythm, vocal timbre, or other distinctive element) as pedagogical bridges toward new learning.

- Explicitly articulate a view that learning music representing diverse cultural traditions is an additive rather than a replacement process. Explain that you'd like to expand students' capabilities by challenging them with new experiences, but that you're not asking them to sacrifice their musical identities or preferences in order to succeed in your ensemble.

- Avoid positioning some musical or cultural traditions as more "valuable" or "legitimate" than others. This requires attending to explicit and implicit messages conveyed to students about the value of each tradition studied, as discussed in Chapter 5.

- Encourage style shifting between vocal timbres and styles appropriate for each cultural tradition studied. Emphasize the appropriateness of vocal timbres and styles for specific cultural and musical contexts rather than treating any style of singing as "correct" in an absolute sense. Approaching vocal timbre and style in this way can support students' view of learning as an additive process, which might in turn encourage their receptivity toward crossing style parameters.

- Choral teachers increasingly collaborate with representatives of specific cultures to provide vocal models for their students, a positive practice that can enhance the cultural validity of those singing experiences. When a given vocal timbre presents a departure from the style of singing with which students are most familiar and comfortable, students may initially (mis)perceive such models as representing unattainable ideals. For that reason, consider also providing vocal models that exemplify successful style shifts. Providing examples of choirs comprised of non-natives to a given culture who successfully approximate a desired vocal timbre and style can illustrate to students that such shifts are attainable with practice and experience. Any such examples should complement rather than replace vocal models contributed by natives of the cultural group represented.

- As part of the classroom's symbolic curriculum, provide images of musicians with diverse cultural identities who perform a range of musical traditions. Include examples of musicians who are proficient style shifters and have achieved success performing in multiple musical traditions.

Multi-Year Spiral Curriculum

The fact that choral teacher-conductors often have the privilege of teaching the same learners for multiple years opens the possibility of transforming the continuum model into a multi-year spiral curriculum:

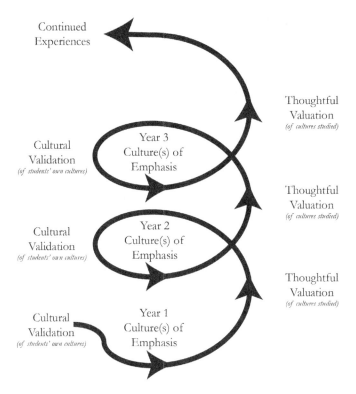

Figure 6.2 Multi-Year Culturally Responsive Spiral Curriculum

Source: © 2012 by National Association for Music Education (formerly MENC). Reprinted with permission.

Note: Figure from Shaw, J. T. (2012). The skin that we sing: Culturally responsive choral music education. *Music Educators Journal*, 98(4), 75–81.

Across several years of participation in a choral ensemble approached in such a way, students would enjoy repeated experiences that promote their own cultural competence while exploring several cultures of emphasis in depth.

Diversifying Curricular Content: Repertoire Selection

Many music specialists gravitate toward diversifying curricular content as an accessible entry point for making their instruction more culturally responsive, a process in which repertoire-related decisions figure prominently. A possible misconception among teachers is that "the repertoire is the curriculum." While repertoire can certainly support a curriculum, it does not in and of itself comprise a curriculum. It is also worth reiterating that including repertoire representing diverse cultural traditions in the curriculum, while an important preliminary step, does not in and of itself accomplish CRT. However, investing effort into making responsible repertoire choices with regard to ways that cultural groups are represented in the curriculum is nevertheless a worthwhile endeavor. Accordingly, this section offers recommendations for selecting repertoire to support a culturally responsive curriculum.

A Person-Centered Approach to Repertoire Selection

Teachers will ideally begin the repertoire selection process by learning more about the backgrounds and identities of specific members of their ensembles and the musical experiences they consider culturally relevant. To inform this process, Gay's (2002) definition of CRT can be transformed into guiding questions:

1. What repertoire would build upon my students' prior experiences?
2. What pieces would capitalize on their cultural knowledge?
3. Through what selections could my students experience through their preferred learning styles?
4. What repertoire would showcase students' culturally informed performance styles?

(Shaw, 2012, p. 76)

Instead of conceptualizing culture as something distant and removed, conductors can attend to the cultural groups represented in their own ensembles as a point of departure for diversifying curricular content.

Evaluating Published Choral Arrangements

Consulting published choral octavos is not the only, and is not necessarily the best, way to locate culturally valid repertoire. If the goal is to select repertoire that is typical and representative of specific cultural groups, beginning by consulting with *people* about repertoire relevant to their cultural backgrounds and identities is often more productive than starting the process with materials such as scores or publisher's catalogues. Additionally, much of the repertoire that would be ideal for exploration in a culturally responsive curriculum would be learned aurally in its culture of origin. Selections drawn from aural traditions can be obtained by consulting with culture bearers either in person or virtually (Goetze, 2000a), or by consulting multimedia resources that can support aural learning experiences (see Box 6.1 for some recommendations).

**Box 6.1: Multimedia Resources to Support Aural
Learning Experiences**

- Books and recordings by Ysaye Barnwell: www.ymbarnwell.com/
  instructional-materials
- The Global Voices in Song series by Mary Goetze. These materials
  are out of print, but may be found in libraries or via third-party
  sellers.
- The Raising the Bar series by Mollie Stone and Patty Cuyler
  and other materials available from The Choral Imperative: www.
  thechoralimperative.com/
- The Vocal Traditions Choral Series and other books with recordings from World Music Press: http://worldmusicpress.com/
  choralseries.php

Conductors are further cautioned that many published choral octavos can
be characterized as "arrangements based upon international material," and
are often created by someone from outside of the culture of origin (Goetze,
2000b, p. 156). It is important, then, to carefully evaluate published materials with an eye toward their cultural validity and the degree to which they
contain cultural bias, which might appear in the form of lyrics or musical
gestures that perpetuate stereotypic thinking (Abril, 2006). One question
helpful for discerning cultural validity is whether cultural insiders would
recognize a given selection as relating to their lived experiences as members of that cultural group, or whether the piece instead offers a distorted,
decontextualized, or stereotypical portrayal. Following are some criteria and
questions intended to be helpful to teacher-conductors as they evaluate the
cultural validity of choral octavos:

1. **Arranger's or editor's credibility.** Is information provided about the
   arranger's or editor's knowledge of the cultural group represented? Have
   they published a piece that held meaning for them personally, having
   experienced it as a member of the cultural group represented? Is the
   publication the result of extensive research carried out with that cultural
   group?
2. **Contextual information**. Is information provided about the historical, social, cultural, and political context in which the piece originated?
   An absence of detail about the arranger's or editor's expertise and cultural context from which the piece originates should raise teachers' sense
   of healthy skepticism. Conduct additional research into the context surrounding the piece, beyond what may be provided in the octavo's inside

cover. If no such information can be located, further investigate the validity of the arrangement or seek an alternative selection.

3. **Recognition of Specific Cultural Communities' Contributions.** Pieces that are vaguely designated as "African folksongs," for example, are problematic in that they portray large groups (e.g., the population of an entire continent; the population of Spanish speakers) as though they are culturally homogenous, glossing over important details of national, ethnic, cultural, or individual identity within those broad populations. Seek pieces in which the contributions of specific national, ethnic, or cultural groups are accurately recognized and represented.

4. **Notation.** Would the piece typically be learned from notation in the culture of origin? If not, what are the qualifications of the person who created the transcription? Be aware that when pieces drawn from aural traditions are transcribed into standard Western notation, important details are often not captured (e.g., stylistic elements, pitches that do not correspond to the twelve-tone chromatic scale, etc.). Additionally, for musicians accustomed to learning Western classical music from notated scores, the very presence of a notated score may cue them to apply stylistic details appropriate for Western classical music whether or not these are appropriate to the culture of origin (Goetze, 2000b).

5. **Reference recordings.** Seek reference recordings generated within the culture of origin, which can be used to track editorial decision-making reflected in notated scores and consider the cultural validity of those decisions.

6. **Instrumentation.** Are suggestions for instrumental parts typical and representative of those that would be used in the culture of origin? Or have they been composed by an educational arranger from outside of the culture?

7. **Text Considerations.** Would members of the culture represented perceive the text as having artistic merit and being worthy of musical interpretation? Too often, educational arrangements marketed as "multicultural selections" are primarily in English with a limited number of words in another language, resulting in a text that is trite or does not meet students' level of sophistication at their current developmental stage (i.e., the text may be simplified to the extent that it resembles something students would have sung as very young children). Seek texts of substance and merit that contribute toward the cultural validity of the selection.

8. **Translation.** Has a translation been provided? Can the accuracy and validity of the translation be discerned? Was the piece's text originally conceptualized in English, but then translated into another language? Has any such translation process reduced the artistic merit or cultural validity of the selection?

9. **Venue.** Is it appropriate to perform the piece in the intended venue? Has the piece originated within a social, cultural, or religious context

in which it would be inappropriate to perform the piece on stage in an auditorium, in a school gym, or another setting outside of the piece's original context?

10. **Context within the performance program.** Does the selection's contextual meaning fit logically within the broader performance program in which it will be featured? Abril (2011) provided an illustrative example of a Mexican-American student who was befuddled by her teacher's decision to perform "*Las Mañanitas*," a song sung in celebration of birthdays, as part of a winter concert program dominated by holiday music. Rather than perceiving the performance as a respectful or meaningful representation of a cultural tradition with which they identified, the student and her family perceived the performance to be odd or nonsensical due to the context within which the piece was performed.

11. **Connection to specific students.** When considering choral repertoire for classroom use, it is important not to lose sight of the learners to whom teachers seek to respond. Students and families can be involved in the process of vetting choral repertoire for possible classroom use. Provide them with the octavo or a recording, and inquire about whether they recognize the piece, whether it is respectfully and accurately represented, and whether they would receive a performance by your choir as being appropriate or relevant.

Consulting With Culture Bearers

For teacher-conductors who are not members of a particular cultural group, it is advisable to consult with a culture bearer throughout the process of selecting, teaching, and performing repertoire representing that group. Such individuals can assist with teaching about the historical, cultural, social, and political context from which repertoire originates. If a piece would be taught orally in its culture of origin, a culture bearer can provide a culturally valid vocal model from whom students can learn aurally. They can coach choirs on matters of performance practice, including singing with appropriate vocal timbre and style and performing movement traditionally associated with the piece.

As teacher-conductors delve into cultural and musical traditions beyond the realm of their personal experience, potential exists for them to unintentionally produce misguided, insensitive, or disrespectful renditions. Potential pitfalls could include using costuming disrespectfully, performing music within an inappropriate venue, and performing movement in ways that could be interpreted as offensive gestures. When missteps such as these occur, public performances can perpetuate cultural misunderstandings, harmful stereotypes, and the very attitudes toward cultural diversity that teachers seek to counteract. A culture bearer can help attenuate such risks by offering honest feedback if our rehearsals or performances veer into inappropriate or disrespectful territory.

Teacher-conductors are urged to remain alert to ways in which culture bearers can be placed in offensive and socially compromising situations. Recognize and respect the fact that requests to "teach about one's culture" can be an exhausting and unwelcome obligation, perhaps especially for members of communities that have experienced marginalization or oppression. If inviting ensemble members to serve as culture bearers, speak with them in advance to ensure that they are willing to serve in that capacity rather than surprising them with such requests mid-rehearsal in front of peers. Avoid positioning individuals as "exotic others" or spokespersons for cultural groups with which they identify. Any guest willing to contribute valuable knowledge and expertise should be respected, recognized, and compensated appropriately. Teacher-conductors can further show respect by preparing thoroughly for collaborations with culture bearers.

Seeking Cultural Validity in Choral Rehearsal and Performance

Cultural validity is enhanced by seeking alignment between discourse norms emphasized in the culture represented, and those through which musical experiences are presented in the classroom. Too often, teachers incorporate content representing diverse cultures and genres into their curricula, yet continue to approach all music through a Western classical pedagogical lens. Some recommendations for attending to cultural validity throughout the process of rehearsal and performance follow, which are paraphrased from Goetze (2000a).

- Whenever possible, foster personal connection between your ensembles and representatives of each culture studied. As Mateo emphasized, the meaning of culturally responsive learning experiences is enhanced by "connecting with actual people, who actually sing the songs."
- If music would be learned aurally in its culture of origin, present it that way in the classroom. If you choose to refer to notation, delay presenting a printed score until students have experienced learning the piece aurally. Then, challenge singers to identify details that are and are not captured in the notated version and shape their performance accordingly.
- Recreate the vocal timbre and style with which the work would be sung in its culture of origin as closely as possible.
- Attend to the integrity with which visual dimensions of the performance are treated, including physical movement and dress.
- Consult with native speakers to ensure accurate pronunciation of languages with which singers are unfamiliar.
- Conduct only when that role is appropriate to the cultural context from which the music originates.
- Enhance the audience's understanding and reception of each piece by providing contextual information through verbal commentary or

program notes. Provided they are willing to serve in this capacity, culture bearers can assist with presenting contextual information to audiences. A personal account of the meaning and significance of a specific piece, as opposed to printed program notes, can foster contextual understandings in an especially vibrant manner for students and audiences alike.

In addition, I recommend the following:

- Consider whether the audience would have a passive, receptive or more active, participatory role in the culture of origin. Seek a venue and performance format that will most closely recreate that dynamic.
- Treat musical preparation for global choral traditions as thoroughly as when preparing a Western classical score for rehearsal or performance. Be prepared to present musical, cultural, and contextual details to students as thoroughly and accurately as possible.

Strive to recreate musical experiences as accurately and faithfully to the culture of origin as possible, attending to each of the previous dimensions of cultural validity. Precise, accurate treatment of the previous elements offers one way to convey genuine respect for each culture studied.

Cultural Congruity in Music Instruction

Teacher-conductors can promote cultural congruity by intentionally aligning the terms of engagement emphasized in our classrooms with ways in which students are knowledgeable, skilled, and experienced as singers and musicians. Following are some recommendations for promoting cultural congruity in choral learning experiences:

- Learn about how students engage with music outside of your choral ensemble. Attend events where students make music, observing the terms of engagement emphasized in those settings. Consider how those terms of engagement could enrich students' experiences within your classroom.
- Provide balanced opportunities for all students to learn aurally and from notation as warranted by each cultural tradition studied. Avoid positioning either of these approaches as superior to the other.
- Inquire about students' preferred vocal models and provide opportunities for them to sing using their preferred performance styles. The cultural responsiveness of a repertoire choice can be undermined if the piece is sung with vocal timbre and style inappropriate to that tradition, leading to students' experiences of cultural incongruity. If providing opportunities for students to perform music that is culturally relevant to them, presenting it with stylistic integrity is essential for students to receive the experience as culturally responsive.

- For students whose cultures of reference emphasize collectivist rather than individualist orientations, competition for chair placements, solos, roles in musicals, and so forth can serve as disenfranchising factors. Cultural responsiveness toward those individuals might entail deemphasizing competition as a discourse norm within the choral organization.

Promoting Sociopolitical Consciousness

Music provides a medium through which students can be guided to recognize and challenge oppression, a process Ladson-Billings (2002) called "promoting students' sociopolitical consciousness" (p. 111). Because of singing's accessibility as a means of expression and the communicative possibilities that lyrics afford, vocal music has long served as a vehicle for sociopolitical commentary. Consequently, choral classrooms provide ideal contexts in which to promote sociopolitical consciousness.

Developing Critical Capacities

Culturally responsive educators aim to develop students' critical capacities, equipping them to recognize and challenge stereotypes, racism, hegemonic structures, and social injustice. Gay (2002) cautioned educators about the powerful influence of a societal curriculum upon students, urging them to actively counter inaccurate, stereotypical, and deficit-laden messages conveyed by media portrayals. Musical media provide an ideal avenue for prompting students' interrogation of the societal curriculum. Students can analyze song lyrics, advertisements, and music videos for ways in which people belonging to social groups related to age, gender, race, ethnicity, socioeconomic status, sexual orientation, and exceptionality are portrayed.

A teacher's first instinct may be to remove all stereotypical or offensive materials from the curriculum. However, to sanitize the curriculum in such a way would risk under-developing students' critical capacities and maintaining, rather than challenging, social injustice. Provided they are developmentally appropriate, such materials can be brought into the classroom for discussion and analysis, supporting students' development of sociopolitical consciousness.

Inquiry Projects Engaging Students in the Role of Social Critic

Engaging students in inquiry projects through which they take on the role of social critic offers another productive means of developing students' sociopolitical consciousness. Options abound for products students can generate from a critical stance, including program notes, opinion pieces, blogs, podcasts, musical compositions, or presentations. Tasked with developing products such as these, students can engage in decision-making about social issues and take action toward resolving them, which corresponds to Banks' (2005) social action approach to multicultural education. Sharing products students develop with a "real audience" beyond the walls of the choral classroom can inspire civic discourse and social action (Kaschub, 2009; McDougall & Trotman, 2011).

Opening Dialogic Spaces

Music can provide an excellent point of departure for discussing, interrogating, and delving deeply into sociocultural and sociopolitical issues. Repertoire drawn from historically significant social movements, such as the United States civil rights movement, the women's suffrage movement, and the South African anti-apartheid movement, to name but a few examples, lends itself well to prompting students' discussion of sociopolitical issues that hold continued relevance. Facilitating classroom dialogue about racism, politics, and additional issues that may arise as students' sociopolitical consciousness develops may initially be a daunting proposition to music teachers, who may be concerned about the potential for such conversations to grow contentious. However, by avoiding or shutting down such conversations, teachers remain implicated in reproducing oppressive systems by silencing the very dialogue that might challenge them (Bradley, 2007; Pollock, 2004). Facilitating such conversations is indeed an ethically complex endeavor that requires thoughtful planning, skilled facilitation, and a systematic approach. Fortunately, authors have developed protocols and guidance for teachers who wish to undertake this important work. While I will not duplicate their efforts, pertinent resources are suggested in the appendix and some recommendations follow.

First, teachers are advised to plan and prepare for classroom discussion just as they would to rehearse a musical score. Developing carefully constructed questions in advance of the discussion is often preferable to generating them on the spot, though teachers must also be prepared to respond flexibly to students' comments in the moment. With experience, teachers can learn to anticipate rhetorical moves students are likely to make and prepare facilitation strategies accordingly.

Consider having students respond to a topic in writing as preparation for subsequent class discussions. Teachers can then consider students' written responses, identify directions subsequent conversations may take, and proactively plan strategies for guiding productive and respectful discourse. Surveys, journaling assignments, exit tickets, and informal conversations with students offer avenues through which teachers can identify social issues students consider worthy of discussion.

When facilitating class discussion about potentially controversial issues, consider using a protocol or framework to guide conversation (see, for example, Clifford, 2015). A protocol outlines a structure for productive dialogue and suggests procedures for equitable turn-taking, respectfully expressing thoughts, receiving other speakers' ideas, and so on. Ensembles can practice using protocols to guide conversation using less controversial topics in order to first build trust, rapport, and a productive process for conversing. Sectional rehearsals may provide a logical context in which to engage in collaborative dialogue. As students gain experience participating in classroom discussions, they can progress toward delving more deeply into sociocultural and sociopolitical issues. After each discussion, reserve time to debrief about how the conversation unfolded. Students can reflect on how well they implemented the protocol, the degree of their engagement, how they navigated any challenges that arose, and the effectiveness with which they discussed the topic.

While teachers' expertise can be valuable in identifying developmentally appropriate topics for discussion and guiding the resulting dialogue, many protocols suggest productive ways for students themselves to initiate and lead discussion. Entrusting students with responsibility for proposing topics and facilitating group conversation aligns well with the student-centered premises of CRT, though this does not mean that teachers abdicate responsibility for providing guidance when needed. It is important to recognize that navigating "courageous conversations" (Singleton & Linton, 2015, p. 7) is a skill students must learn and practice, just as they learn to collaborate on musical endeavors.

Connecting Musical Involvement With Civic Discourse and Social Action

Students' process of developing sociopolitical consciousness encompasses not only developing the critical capacities necessary to recognize and challenge oppression, but also taking action toward solving social issues of importance to them. Although the precise link between musical experiences and social change can seem nebulous, prompting civic discourse is one way that musical involvement can potentially lead to social action.

Abril (2011) described one such example in which a teacher developed a mariachi program in an effort to respond to her school's growing Hispanic population. A tension arose when students questioned one of the teacher's repertoire choices, *"La Raspa"* ("The Mexican Hat Dance"), which they considered offensive because of its stereotypical portrayal of Mexican culture. Rather than becoming defensive, the teacher tasked students with conducting a survey of community members, analyzing the responses, and using them to inform the ensemble's decision regarding whether to continue learning the piece. This example is noteworthy in that dialogue the teacher encouraged extended beyond the classroom walls, prompting discourse in the community at large. Of further note is the way the teacher viewed her role, not as the sole authority on all artistic decision-making, but as a teacher willing to learn from and alongside students.

Kristy, a participant in a yet-to-be published study of urban music educators' culturally responsive practice (Shaw, in press) provided an additional example of a musical performance connected with civic discourse. Students at her predominately African American school participated in a community event in which their choral performance complemented a presentation on the topic of school segregation. The choir performed selections from the U.S. civil rights movement including "Ain't Gonna Let Nobody Turn Me Round" and "People Get Ready." The guest speaker prompted the audience to question why the predominately African American school choir featured on stage was not reflective of the demographic diversity present in the broader community. She presented research on school resegregation, after which attendees participated in an open-mic community dialogue. Community members, including choir students, proposed a range of concrete actions for addressing the issue within their city. Students observed how their musical involvement served as a catalyst for civic discourse about a sociopolitical issue of importance in their community and the nation at large.

To help students identify possibilities for social action, choral directors can foster interaction with individuals holding power to affect social change. Kaschub (2009) documented one such example in which students created musical compositions that commented on social issues of importance to them. Government officials, relief workers, and representatives from local charities and community agencies attended the premiere performances of students' compositions. By inviting such individuals to interface directly with students, the teacher created a discernable link between musical involvement and social action.

Underexplored Territory and Future Possibilities for CRT

Teachers' and students' perspectives shed light on underexplored possibilities for CRT that could inform future research and practice. These include using creative engagements such an improvisation and composition as avenues for CRT, responding to facets of students' cultural identities in addition to race and ethnicity, and responding to political dimensions of students' lived experiences. This section describes each of these possibilities further in relation to pertinent literature.

Creative Engagements as Avenues for CRT

Creative musical engagements, including composition and improvisation, are conducive to pursuing the aims of CRT (Hickey, 2008; Kaschub, 2009; Smith, 2014), yet these possibilities remain underexplored in many choral classrooms. Student contributors to this book enjoyed creating their own music outside of their choral ensembles, potential that remained untapped by their teachers. Music they created frequently served as a vehicle for social commentary. For example, Zoey's impetus for composing was to express "what goes on in the world," and to comment on "things that are and are not right in life."

Creative musical engagements open possibilities for circumventing barriers to CRT presented by a repertoire-centric approach, limitations of which are discussed elsewhere in this volume. Rather than solely performing music conceived by others, students can explore and express their own artistic voices via improvisation and composition, a process conducive to promoting cultural competence. Composition affords students control over which facets of their identities to express artistically and in what manner, attenuating the possibility that misguided teacher assumptions about students' identities will result in alienating learning experiences for them. Instructional time invested into composition projects can simultaneously promote cultural competence for all of the individuals in the classroom, no matter how large or culturally diverse.

Music students consider relevant to their cultural identities can be brought into the classroom and used as models for students' creative inspiration (Hickey, 2008; Kaschub, 2009; Smith, 2014). One challenge teachers frequently cite as they attempt CRT is that students' culturally relevant musical models may feature lyrics or subject matter inappropriate for exploration in school contexts. Further, some music students consider culturally relevant may include stylistic features that do not readily translate to the medium of choral performance. Rather than rejecting such selections outright as being "inappropriate," teachers can encourage students to compose in the style of those models, taking the intended audience and context for reception into account.

Musical composition also offers a medium for students to artistically voice their perspectives on social issues of importance to them, opening possibilities for fostering sociopolitical consciousness. When encouraging students to discuss, analyze, and take action toward solving social issues of importance to them, one ethical dilemma teachers frequently cite is how to avoid imposing one's own perspective upon students. Composing locates artistic agency with students, allowing them to comment on social issues from their own perspective without undue influence from the teacher or other individuals.

Merely engaging students in improvisation or composition is insufficient for developing sociopolitical consciousness, which depends on opportunities for critical analysis surrounding the creative process. As students consider what makes model compositions effective, they can learn to recognize and challenge stereotypes, especially in their manifestations as musical clichés. Listening circles, in which students share works in progress (Smith, 2014), can serve as dialogic spaces for prompting students' critical analysis of sociopolitical issues. Sharing students' works with an audience beyond the classroom walls can create links between music and civic discourse (Kaschub, 2009), allowing students to envision how composing music could ultimately inspire social change.

Creative musical engagements can complement performance-based experiences while supporting culturally responsive practice. Investing time in even one composition project each year can productively foster students' cultural competence, sociopolitical consciousness, and artistic agency. Readers are encouraged to consult Hickey (2012), Kerchner and Strand (2016), and Upitis (1992) for practical advice on guiding composition experiences for students. Additional relevant resources are recommended in the appendix.

Responding to Facets of Students' Identities in Addition to Race and Ethnicity

This book, like much of the extant literature on CRT, has focused primarily on how race and ethnicity mediate students' music learning experiences. However, additional facets of cultural identity, including age, gender, socioeconomic status, sexual orientation, and exceptionality hold implications for what experiences constitute culturally responsive instruction for each individual. While the scope of this book precluded in-depth exploration of each of these elements, teachers are encouraged to consider how their pedagogy can respond to these additional facets of students' identities, as well as intersections between them (see Crenshaw, 1989). Pertinent resources are suggested in the appendix.

Politically Relevant Teaching

Some authors have emphasized the sociopolitical consciousness component of CRT to the extent that they have suggested that CRT might more appropriately be termed *politically* relevant teaching. This is not to suggest that teachers should impose views related to partisan politics upon children, but that teachers can take political dimensions of students' lived experiences into account in order to educate them more effectively. For example, Beauboeuf-Lafontant (1999) observed:

> Regardless of their culture of origin, culturally relevant teachers appear to share an understanding of systemic inequity—that is, the political, economic, and racial structures that disproportionately limit the opportunities of children of color. . . . These teachers are mindful not only of the cultural norms, values, and practices of their students, but more importantly of the political realities and aspirations of people of color. As a result, their pedagogy is "relevant" to the *political* experiences of inequity and disenfranchisement of their students.
>
> (pp. 704–705)

The notion of politically relevant teaching was particularly salient within the South Side Choir, where students' positive reception of repertoire Mr. Mitchell selected, classroom discussions he guided, and learning experiences he facilitated often related to the political relevance of classroom activities to their lived experiences. Scholars have also emphasized teachers' explicit acknowledgment of and action toward dismantling racism and systemic inequity as being foundational to the practice of CRT (Hyland, 2005; Lehmberg, 2008; Villegas & Lucas, 2002). Continued inquiry into political dimensions of CRT, and ways in which teachers can ethically practice politically relevant teaching, would be informative to scholars and practitioners alike.

Beauboeuf-Lafontant further asserted, "focusing our attention on the political rather than cultural experiences of students provides us with a way of productively engaging with the reality of a majority White female teaching force educating an increasingly non-White public school population" (p. 719), an assertion as relevant presently as when originally written. Thus, teachers of all sociocultural backgrounds can be encouraged that an ability to engage in CRT is not solely dependent upon teachers' shared cultural commonalities with students. Rather, teachers of any background who commit to investing the requisite effort can develop knowledge, skills, and dispositions necessary to effectively educate students through culturally and politically relevant pedagogy.

This book has explored pedagogical possibilities for making choral music education more responsive to cultural diversity, drawing on the perspectives of three teachers and nine students of differing ethnicities. The fact that CRT evolves in response to particular students' cultural backgrounds, identities, and learning needs precludes the possibility of offering a definitive "how-to" guide that can guarantee culturally responsive practice with any students in any context. The specific curriculum designs, learning experiences, and repertoire choices described in this volume may not readily transfer to additional learners or educational settings. However, overarching principles and guiding questions raised by the teachers' and students' experiences can inform teachers' work to develop CRT for their own learners.

There is no endpoint at which a teacher can be declared a fully evolved culturally responsive teacher. Rather, the journey toward cultural responsiveness is continuous, requiring ongoing critical self-reflection about one's own cultural identity, how culture shapes one's approach to teaching, how that approach is aligned or misaligned with students' orientations toward education, and one's own implication in social and educational inequity. The process requires continual effort to develop detailed knowledge of students' cultural backgrounds, identities, perspectives, lived experiences, strengths, and learning needs and to translate that knowledge into pedagogical action. Cultural responsiveness further demands teachers' ongoing commitment to acting as change agents within schools and communities, actively working to dismantle inequitable and oppressive structures that limit the opportunities of students from non-dominant communities.

Learning about and adopting CRT is unlikely unfold in a smooth and predictable manner. The process will likely encompass epiphanies and positive progress on some occasions intermingled with missteps, upended assumptions, and unanticipated challenges on others. Evolving as a culturally responsive teacher is also likely to include intense personal and professional growth, which may not always be comfortable. Yet, for teachers willing to undertake this important work, the potential benefits to students are profound. Through culturally responsive choral pedagogy, teachers can provide more equitable access to music education opportunities; engage students in meaningful, relevant instruction; affirm singers' evolving cultural and musical identities; and support students' efforts to catalyze positive change in society. Because choral pedagogy can be approached in a way that honors the uniqueness of each human voice, choral educators are well-positioned to teach in ways that are responsive to individual students' cultural heritages and identities.

References

Abril, C. R. (2006). Music that represents culture: Selecting music with integrity. *Music Educators Journal*, *93*(1), 38–45. https://doi.org/10.1177/002743210609300122

Abril, C. R. (2009). Responding to culture in the instrumental music programme: A teacher's journey. *Music Education Research*, *11*(1), 77–91. https://doi.org/10.1080/14613800802699176

Abril, C. R. (2011). Opening spaces in the instrumental music classroom. In A. Clements (Ed.), *Alternative approaches to music education* (pp. 3–14). Lanham, MD: Rowman & Littlefield.

Banks, J. A. (2005). Approaches to multicultural curriculum reform. In J. A. Banks & C. A. M. Banks (Eds.), *Multicultural education: Issues and perspectives* (5th ed., pp. 242–261). Hoboken, NJ: Wiley.

Beauboeuf-Lafontant, T. (1999). A movement against and beyond boundaries: "Politically relevant teaching" among African American teachers. *Teachers College Record*, *100*(4), 702–723.

Bradley, D. (2007). The sounds of silence: Talking race in music education. *Action, Criticism & Theory for Music Education*, *6*(4), 132–162.

Carlow, R. (2004). *Hearing others' voices: An exploration of the music experience of immigrant students who sing in high school choir* (Doctoral dissertation). Retrieved from ProQuest Dissertations & Theses. (AAT 3152852).

Clifford, A. (2015). *Teaching restorative practices with classroom circles*. Santa Rosa, CA: Center for Restorative Process.

Crenshaw, K. (1989). Demarginalizing the intersection of race and sex: A black feminist critique of antidiscrimination doctrine, feminist theory and antiracist politics. *University of Chicago Legal Forum*, *1*(8), 139–167.

Delpit, L. D. (1995). *Other people's children: Cultural conflict in the classroom*. New York, NY: Norton.

Dewey, J. (1925). *Experience and nature*. Chicago, IL: Open Court Publishing Company.

Gay, G. (2002). Preparing for culturally responsive teaching. *Journal of Teacher Education*, *53*(2), 106–116.

Goetze, M. (2000a). Challenges of performing diverse cultural music. *Music Educators Journal*, *87*(1), 23–25, 48.

Goetze, M. (2000b). The challenges of performing choral music of the world. In B. F. Reimer (Ed.), *Performing with understanding: The challenge of the national standards for music education* (pp. 155–169). Reston, VA: MENC.

Hickey, M. (2008). At-risk teens: Making sense of life through music composition. In J. L. Kerchner & C. R. Abril (Eds.), *Musical experience in our lives: Things we learn and meanings we make* (pp. 201–217). Lanham, MD: Rowman & Littlefield.

Hickey, M. (2012). *Music outside the lines: Ideas for composing in K-12 classrooms.* New York, NY: Oxford University Press.

Hyland, N. E. (2005). Being a good teacher of black students? White teachers and unintentional racism. *Curriculum Inquiry, 35*(4), 429–459.

Kaschub, M. (2009). Critical pedagogy for creative artists: Inviting young composers to engage in artistic social action. In E. Gould, J. Countryman, C. Morton, & L. Stewart Rose (Eds.), *Exploring social justice: How music education might matter* (pp. 289–306). Toronto, ON: Canadian Music Educators' Association.

Kelly-McHale, J. (2011). *The relationship between children's musical identities and music teacher beliefs and practices in an elementary general music classroom* (Doctoral dissertation). Retrieved from ProQuest Dissertations & Theses. (AAT 3456672).

Kerchner, J. L., & Strand, K. (2016). *Musicianship: Composing in choir.* Chicago, IL: GIA Publications.

Ladson-Billings, G. J. (1994). *The dream-keepers: Successful teachers of African American children.* San Francisco, CA: Jossey-Bass.

Ladson-Billings, G. J. (2002). I ain't writin' nuttin': Permissions to fail and demands to succeed in urban classrooms. In L. D. Delpit & J. K. Dowdy (Eds.), *The skin that we speak: Thoughts on language and culture in the classroom* (pp. 107–120). New York, NY: Norton.

Lehmberg, L. J. (2008). *Perceptions of effective teaching and pre-service preparation for urban elementary general music classrooms: A study of teachers of different cultural backgrounds in various cultural settings* (Doctoral dissertation). Retrieved from ProQuest Dissertations & Theses. (AAT 3326036).

McDougall, J., & Trotman, D. (2011). Real audience pedagogy: Creative learning and digital space. In J. Sefton-Green, P. Thomson, K. Jones, & L. Bresler (Eds.), *The Routledge international handbook of creative learning* (pp. 273–282). New York, NY: Routledge.

Mostern, K. (1994). Decolonization as learning: Practice and pedagogy in Frantz Fanon's revolutionary narrative. In H. Giroux & P. McLaren (Eds.), *Between borders: Pedagogy and the politics of cultural studies* (pp. 253–271). New York, NY: Routledge.

Pollock, M. (2004). *Colormute: Race talk dilemmas in an American school.* Princeton, NJ: Princeton University Press.

Shaw, J. T. (2012). The skin that we sing: Culturally responsive choral music education. *Music Educators Journal, 98*(4), 75–81. https://doi.org/10.1177/0027432112443561

Shaw, J. T. (in press). Urban music educators' perceived professional growth in a context-specific professional development program. *Journal of Research in Music Education.*

Singleton, G. E., & Linton, C. W. (2015). *Courageous conversations about race: A field guide for achieving equity in schools* (2nd ed.). Thousand Oaks, CA: Corwin.

Smith, J. P. (2014). Spaces for student voices: Composition in schools and issues of social justice. In J. R. Barrett & P. R. Webster (Eds.), *The musical experience: Rethinking music teaching and learning* (pp. 149–166). New York, NY: Oxford University Press.

Thibeault, M. D. (2009). The violin and the fiddle: Narratives of music and musician in a high-school setting. In C. R. Abril & J. L. Kerchner (Eds.), *Musical experience in our lives: Things we learn and meanings we make* (pp. 255–276). Lanham, MD: Rowman & Littlefield.

Upitis, R. (1992). *Can I play you my song?: The compositions and invented notations of children.* Portsmouth, NH: Heinemann.

Villegas, A. M., & Lucas, T. (2002). Preparing culturally responsive teachers: Rethinking the curriculum. *Journal of Teacher Education, 53*(1), 20–32. https://doi.org/10.1177/0022487102053001003

Appendix
Selected Resources to Support CRT

Selecting Culturally Valid Repertoire

Abril, C. R. (2006). Music that represents culture: Selecting music with integrity. *Music Educators Journal, 93*(1), 38–45.

Performing Choral Music Representing Diverse Choral Traditions With Integrity

Goetze, M. (2000). Challenges of performing diverse cultural music. *Music Educators Journal, 87*(1), 23–25, 48.

Goetze, M. (2000). The challenges of performing choral music of the world. In B. F. Reimer (Ed.), *Performing with understanding: The challenge of the national standards for music education* (pp. 155–169). Reston, VA: MENC.

Parr, C. (2006). Eight simple rules for singing multicultural music. *Music Educators Journal, 93*(1), 34–37.

Ethically Approaching Conversations About Race, Politics, and Additional Issues in Schools

Clifford, A. (2015). *Teaching restorative practices with classroom circles.* Santa Rosa, CA: Center for Restorative Process.

Pollock, M. (2017). *Schooltalk: Rethinking what we say about—and to—students.* New York, NY: The New Press.

Singleton, G. E., & Linton, C. W. (2015). *Courageous conversations about race: A field guide for achieving equity in schools* (2nd ed.). Thousand Oaks, CA: Corwin.

Willoughby, B. (2012). *Speak up at school: How to respond to everyday prejudice, bias, and stereotypes, a guide for teachers.* Montgomery, AL: Southern Poverty Law Center. Retrieved from www.tolerance.org/sites/default/files/general/Speak_Up_at_School.pdf

Exploring Musical Composition as an Avenue for CRT

Hickey, M. (2008). At-risk teens: Making sense of life through music composition. In J. L. Kerchner & C. R. Abril (Eds.), *Musical experience in our lives: Things we learn and meanings we make* (pp. 201–217). Lanham, MD: Rowman & Littlefield.

Kaschub, M. (2009). Critical pedagogy for creative artists: Inviting young composers to engage in artistic social action. In E. Gould, J. Countryman, C. Morton, &

L. Stewart Rose (Eds.), *Exploring social justice: How music education might matter* (Vol. 4, pp. 289–306). Toronto, ON: Canadian Music Educators' Association.

Smith, J. P. (2014). Spaces for student voices: Composition in schools and issues of social justice. In J. R. Barrett & P. R. Webster (Eds.), *The musical experience: Rethinking music teaching and learning* (pp. 149–166). New York, NY: Oxford University Press.

Shaw, J. T. (2016). Student composers as change agents: Socially just and culturally responsive music education through composition. In J. L. Kerchner & K. D. Strand (Eds.), *Musicianship: Composing in choir* (pp. 63–82). Chicago, IL: G.I.A. Publications.

Responsiveness to Facets of Cultural Identity in Addition to Race and Ethnicity

Bergonzi, L. (2009). Sexual orientation and music education. *Music Educators Journal*, *96*(2), 21–25.

Darrow, A.-A. (2013). Culturally responsive teaching: Understanding disability culture. *General Music Today*, *26*(3), 32–34.

Palkki, J., & Caldwell, P. (2017). "We are often invisible": A survey on safe space for LGBTQ students in secondary school choral programs. *Research Studies in Music Education*, *40*(1), 28–49.

Palkki, J. (2015). Gender trouble: Males, adolescence, and masculinity in the choral context. *Choral Journal*, *56*(4), 24–35.

Palkki, J. (2017). Inclusivity in action: Transgender students in the choral classroom. *Choral Journal*, *57*(11), 20–34.

Sweet, B., & Parker, E. C. (2019). Female vocal identity development: A phenomenology. *Journal of Research in Music Education*, *67*(1), 62–82.

Shaw, J. T. (2017). Toward socially inclusive music organizations: Promoting socioeconomic diversity in choral ensembles. *Choral Journal*, *58*(4), 22–36.

Sieck, S. (2017). *Teaching with respect: Inclusive pedagogy for choral directors.* Milwaukee, WI: Hal Leonard.

Index

Printed in the United States
by Baker & Taylor Publisher Services